New York

New York

By Simon Gage

Thomas
Cook
Publishing

The
Pink Paper

Published by Thomas Cook Publishing
PO Box 227
The Thomas Cook Business Park
Coningsby Road
Peterborough
PE3 8XX

Email: books@thomascook.com

ISBN: 1841571 628

Text © 2002 Thomas Cook Publishing
Maps and photographs © 2002 Thomas Cook Publishing

For Thomas Cook Publishing
Managing Director: Kevin Fitzgerald
Publisher: Donald Greig
Commissioning Editor: Deborah Parker
Editors: Sarah Hudson, Jane Egginton
Proofreader: Ian Kearey

For Pink Paper
General Manager: David Bridle
Publishing Manager: Mike Ross
Editor: Steve Anthony
Additional picture research: Claire Benjamin

Design: Studio 183 and Grassverge
Layout: Studio 183, Peterborough
Cover Design: Studio 183 and Grassverge
Cover Artwork: Steve Clarke, Studio 183

City maps drawn by: Steve Munns
Transport maps: Transport Cartographic Service

Scanning: Dale Carrington, Chronos Publishing; David Bruce Graphics

Printed and bound in Spain by: Artes Gráficas Elkar, Loiu, Spain

Written and researched by Simon Gage

Photography: Mark O'Flaherty

Additional photography:
Amanda Lehner: pages 14 (Grand Central), 24 (NYSE), 25, 31, 35 (Burritos), 36 (St
Mark's), 53 (Whitney), 74, 75, 99.

The following are thanked for supplying photographs, to whom the copyright belongs:
Brasserie: pages 78, 98.
Ethel Davies: pages 18, 53 (Guggenheim), 61, 66, 144.
Hudson Hotel/Michael Mundy: pages 92, 119, 121.
The Museum of Modern Art: page 15 (Les Demoiselles d'Avignon by Pablo Picasso).
Neil Setchfield: pages 41 (browsing), 65, 108, 114.
Soho Grand: page 122.

Cover photographs:
Main photograph: Nigel Francis/Robert Harding.com
Other photographs: Mark O'Flaherty, Scott Nunn

Contents

CONTENTS

My Kind of Town...

I may not be a native New Yorker, but who is? And I've done my time, up in Harlem and down on Broadway.

In fact, over the last 12 or so years I've pretty much covered the bases in NYC. I've lived out my *Village People* fantasies at the rough and ready YMCA, and my *Sex and the City* fantasies at the fabulous Soho Grand. I've holed up on the Upper West Side in boutique hotels and down on the Lower East Side in rent-controlled slums where mice and cockroaches patrolled the laundry room. I've taken my life in my hands scouring the meatpacking district to find a quirky club with Deborah Harry in full crinolines, and I've taken my finances in my hand cruising the world's best stores with a fully-functioning credit card. And I've loved every minute of it, even if New York can sometimes seem like a noisy, aggressive stress factory.

During those 12 years of going back and back and back – sometimes to write about it, sometimes to just live it – I've seen New York change from a dirty, dangerous place, where riding the subway was always just a heartbeat away from turning into an episode of *Cagney and Lacey* and stumbling onto 42nd Street was like entering an open-air crack house, into a civilised city where you can pretty much go where you like as long as you're keeping half a New York eye out. New Yorkers still love to bang on about how it's the grittiest city in the world, but I've travelled all over the world writing travel features, and there are far dodgier places than Manhattan.

This guide is not intended to review every last Starbucks on every last street corner. It's supposed to point you in the direction of the most fun you can have in the most fun place on earth, a place where you can spend the morning looking at the world's most famous works of art and taking in the finest views known to civilisation, and the evening going to one of the world's best clubs.

Simon Gage would like to thank Eric Charge, Lisa Richards and Anna Lawson.

New York – skyscrapers and steam

Out in New York

Well, if you can't be gay in New York, where can you be gay?

It is, after all, the birthplace of gay liberation, the city where gay men first organised themselves and started to fight back against victimisation by the police. It's a long (and great) story, but the bottom line is the cops chose to bust the Stonewall Bar down in the Village one night back in 1969 and, having had enough of this kind of thing, the gay men and drag queens in there decided to fight them right back. It was just a couple of nights of trouble but, more importantly, it was the first time the idea of a 'gay community' had come up. And everyone kind of liked it.

Even before Stonewall, New York had always been a magnet for gay men. Not only is it the most sophisticated and adventurous city in what is still a very conservative and religious country, but its sheer size has always meant that the gay boy from Ohio at last felt free to do whatever he wanted without having to worry that it would get back to his folks. Add to that the fact that it's a total melting pot of races, colours, creeds and characters, and you soon understand that gay people have been accepted – or ignored, which is often better – in a way that is almost unique in the United States.

But it's not all been one-way traffic. New York got the way it is because of the input of gay men and lesbians and drag queens and, well, our kind of people. The intellectual atmosphere has a lot to do with us, as does the art scene, the club scene, the restaurant scene, pretty much every scene come to think of it. And you don't get that sort of thriving theatrical community without a good proportion of gay men in the mix.

But just because Lady Liberty has been holding a torch for gay men from all over the world, just because it's the city of Truman Capote and Andy Warhol and Robert Mapplethorpe and Keith Haring and just about every other key gay mover and shaker from the last century, it doesn't mean you can throw caution to the wind and just go about your gay old business without a care in the world.

In a city where the vibe can change from street to street, it's just as well to keep your wits about you. Homophobia is still out there, and even though New Yorkers have been brought up to expect anything, they've not necessarily been brought up to accept everything. Gay bashing has always gone on and, while levels of violence have plummeted in New York, some neighbourhoods are still more or less no-go areas for anyone, let alone a couple of beautifully turned out gay boys

Frills and fashions

ticket, went overboard. He outlawed any gay activity he found unacceptable even, according to some reports, paying spies to go into gay clubs in order to rat on them to the authorities. The result is that what was once the wildest city on earth for gay men has become a shadow of its former self, with racy clubs toned down beyond recognition and certain sections of the party circuit closed down completely. There is still go-go action; there are even strip joints and the odd raunchy club; but anyone who revelled in the decadence of the 1970s, when the scene was as 'out there' as scenes can possibly get, will be sorely disappointed. In fact, anyone who has been out on the scene in Europe, will find the sexy side of New York a bit on the tame side. It's certainly no longer the town where anything goes.

swishing along with a clutch of Dolce & Gabbana bags. As in most cities, gay men don't really flaunt it by holding hands or making obvious displays of affection. If you insist on giving your partner a tweak, make sure you're doing it within the confines of Chelsea, the designated gay neighbourhood, and even there proceed with caution. New York has more than its fair share of have-a-go locals, most of them operating in the name of the Lord.

Despite the odd pockets of homophobia, New York as a city has been forced to take its gay citizens (and visitors) seriously. New York Gay Pride is huge, with figures running into millions and major politicians scrabbling to get on that stage to show their support. (But the St Patrick's Day Parade is different – they still won't let gay men and lesbians on that.)

It's not all sunshine and roses for gay people in New York, even if we have wangled ourselves a fair bit of clout. The recently replaced Mayor Rudy Giuliani, who was elected on a clean-up-the-city

The clampdown on public partying was partly justified by the huge impact of AIDS from the early 1980s on. Apart from claiming the lives of huge swathes of gay party people, the people most intent on enjoying the freedom they had won that night at the Stonewall, AIDS had the effect of re-politicising the gay community, with groups like ACT UP, and creating a support network for the growing HIV community. There are now great pharmacies that make the whole palaver of buying and taking your HIV drugs a relatively pleasant experience.

AIDS also had the effect of promoting the whole 'Look, I'm healthy' gay obsession with the gym body, which still dominates the New York scene.

New York is still a Mecca for gay men. The clubs can be mind-blowing and are certainly varied. You can be in a Latino drag club one night, a hardcore techno bar the next – and the 'lounge' phenomenon (it's a halfway house between bar and club) is still growing with the opening of joints like XL proving that there's life in Chelsea yet.

There's certainly no shortage of free gay press in New York, from weekly bar magazine *HX* through *Metro*, which is so nicely put together you can't believe it's free, to *HIV Plus* and the more serious

gay newspapers. *Time Out New York* has a gay section, while the legendary *Village Voice* – now also free and available from stands in the street – has a very strong gay flavour, with columnist Michael Musto providing the very latest word on the New York scene. Check it out online before you go: on www.villagevoice.com. In a scene that changes with the weather, you've got to make sure you're up to date.

New York City has pretty much everything you need for a happy gay holiday – exciting shops, buzzing bars, happening clubs and plenty of glamour everywhere you go. All you need to do is get yourself in a New York state of mind. This guide is the perfect place to start.

Nights on Broadway

Welcoming all to the city

Stepping Out

The strange thing about New York City is that you feel as though you've been there before, even if you've never set foot in the US. But that doesn't mean that sights such as the Empire State and the Brooklyn Bridge can't still knock you for six, even from a distance.

My Top Sights

Brooklyn Bridge

Subway J, M, Z to Chambers Street or 4, 5, 6 to Brooklyn Bridge-City Hall   Admission free

One of the most famous crossing points in the world, the Brooklyn Bridge links Manhattan to Brooklyn at the southeast end of the island. By far New York City's most

Gateway to Manhattan

beautiful bridge, the twin Gothic arches are the most fantastic gateway to the city and, when it was completed in 1883, it was the world's longest suspension bridge. Take the A or C train over to Brooklyn and then wander on the wooden walkway back to Manhattan and take in the views. Remember your camera, as there are some devilish shots to be had of the bridge's steel cables with the immense skyscrapers of lower Manhattan in the background. (*See map p. 20*)

Central Park

Between 59th and 110th Streets, Central Park West (8th Avenue) and 5th Avenue   Subway A, B, C, D, 1, 9 to 59th Street-Columbus Circle; or N, R to 5th Avenue; alternatively, Subway B, C to 81st Street, W 96th Street or Cathedral Parkway

A city in itself, these 86 acres are so familiar from a whole variety of films, you'll feel like you've been to Central Park before you set foot in it.

Take it easy in Central Park

See the lanes Woody Allen is always leading some unsuspecting young girl down, the bridge where Shirley Maclaine got pushed in the boating lake in *Sweet Charity*, the ice-skaters you've seen against the backdrop of chunky South Park buildings a million times. There's plenty to see and do here. You can take a gondola out on the water, walk through the Ramble, eat in the upmarket Tavern on the Green restaurant, see concerts and Shakespeare plays. Alternatively, you could just relax and watch the rollerbladers whizz by, or lie on the grass topping up your tan with the other gay men at Sheep's Meadow. (*See map p. 50*)

Empire State Building

ℹ 34th Street-Herald Square
☏ 212-736-3100 www.esbnyc.com
☼ Observatories 9.30am–11.30pm
Ⓜ Subway B, D, F, Q, N, R to 34th Street
$ $7, cash only

Art Deco tower

One of the most famous buildings in the world, the Empire State Building was the tallest construction ever built when it was completed in 1931. At over a quarter of a mile high, it has lost none of its power to excite, especially when glimpsed from a bus window on the way from the airport or when it's lit up for special occasions, including a lovely lilac for Gay Pride. Travel up this beautifully Art Deco granite tower for panoramic views of the city by catching an elevator to the 86th floor and, if you can bear the queues, the 102nd. (*See map p. 44*)

Stunning station

Grand Central Station

ℹ 42nd to 44th Streets between Vanderbilt and Lexington Avenues
Ⓜ Subway S, 4, 5, 6, 7 to 42nd Street-Grand Central
$ Admission free

Okay, so you can list the films it's been in, but

until you stand on the giant concourse, you'll never get a true sense of its enormity and beauty. The refurbishment of this cathedral-like building was completed in 1998 and is stunning inside and out. Make sure you look up in the concourse area and catch a glimpse of the beautifully painted ceiling, and don't forget the Oyster Bar. (*See map p. 44*)

Les Demoiselles d'Avignon – Picasso

MoMA QNS

🛈 45–20 33rd Street at Queens Boulevard, Long Island City

📞 212-708-9400 www.moma.org

🕐 Mon, Tues, Thu, Sat 10.30am–5.45pm; Fri 10.30am–8.15pm 🚇 Subway 7 Local to 33rd Street 💲 $10

Obviously, you can't ignore the Metropolitan Museum of Art, the Whitney or the Guggenheim, but for sheer novelty value you have to check out the Museum of Modern Art now it's relocated to an industrial building in the borough of Queens while its beautiful 53rd Street building gets a billion-dollar facelift. It's an adventure as well as being an interesting train journey out of Manhattan. (*See map p. 64*)

Rockefeller Center

🛈 48th to 51st Street between 5th and 6th Avenues

📞 212-632-3975

🚇 Subway B, D, F, Q to 47-50th Streets-Rockefeller Centre 💲 Admission free

Prometheus keeps an eye on the plaza

The 11-acre art deco complex known simply as Rockefeller, with its 19 public buildings at the heart of Midtown, is an enormous public space loved by Manhattanites. Tours of the legendary NBC television studios take place daily, while in the winter months the central gardens boast that famous outdoor skating rink and enormous Christmas tree. Check out the beautiful Art Deco features, wander into the shiny lobbies to check out hidden pieces of art, and abuse your credit card in the many shops. (*See map p. 44*)

STEPPING OUT

Statue of Liberty

ℹ️ Liberty Island Ferry from Battery Park

📞 212-363-3200

www.ellisisland.org

🕐 9.15am–3.30pm

🚇 Subway N, R to Whitehall Street or 1, 9 to South Ferry or 4, 5 to Bowling Green

🎫 Return ferry ticket, includes entry to Liberty Island and Ellis Island Museum, $7

Miss Liberty

The Statue of Liberty *is* New York, so it's no wonder nearly six million people a year flock to see the green lady with the torch. This is why it's not exactly the best idea in the world to waste precious hours hanging around waiting to climb for a view, which, in a city of breathtaking views, is shortlived. You'll be hustled round that crown and have to look through thick, scratched-up glass. Besides, in an effort to preserve the Lady, they have started limiting tickets to the crown to the first ferry during the peak season. The Immigration Museum on Ellis Island is worth a look, but the best way to view Lady Liberty is undoubtedly from the Staten Island Ferry or from the corny-sounding but incredibly romantic Circle Line boat tour (from Pier 83, 42nd Street at 12th Avenue; 212-563-3200 www.circleline.com). Go at sunset, and there'll be a tear in your eye. Alternatively, splash out on a helicopter ride. (*See map p. 20*)

Times Square

ℹ️ 42nd Street at Broadway

🚇 Subway N, R, S, 1, 2, 3, 7, 9 to Times Square-42nd Street

Considering you've heard about it all your life, you might find Times Square a bit of a let-down. Yes, the neons are amazing – especially the Nasdaq Center, a building that doubles up as a screen – but the tourists are horrendous and there's nothing much to see or do unless you're taking in a blockbusting

Times Square

musical or shopping at the Virgin Megastore. But you have to see it just to say you have. (*See map p. 44*)

Washington Square

ℹ Between 4th Street and Waverly Place
Ⓜ Subway A, C, E, B, D, F, Q to W 4th
Street

Singing in the Square

If you ever get tired of the new-
ness and sheer verticality of New
York, the area around Washington
Square will give you a bit of a
break. The hub of New York
University has buildings that are
comfortingly antique, while the greenery and strangely coloured
squirrels should help you chill out. You'll recognise the iconic memorial
arch from many famous films. (*See map p. 34*)

World Trade Center

When terrorists flew hijacked planes into the World Trade
Center on 11th September 2001, New York was changed
forever. Apart from the huge loss of human life, the greatest
city on earth just didn't feel quite as invulnerable any more. And
physically, the most famous skyline in the world was missing its
star players. Because the World Trade Center's Twin Towers were
not just skyscrapers. They were geographical pointers, something
every New Yorker looked towards to get their bearings, to
check what the weather was like, to catch a great sunset
reflected in the 100-and-odd storeys. But more than just high –
and they were so high, literally cloud-scrapingly high – the
Twin Towers were beautiful, more like jewellery than
architecture. Where the Empire State is beautiful from afar but
close up looks pretty much like, well, a building up close, the
Twin Towers of the World Trade Center were pristine and
sparkling and sleek, easily the most beautiful buildings in the
city, and an obvious choice when I was picking my top sights.

Now they have been replaced by a crater that extends for
two blocks, an area that for years will be nothing more than a
gruesome reminder of what used to be, and frankly not helped
by the grotesque spectacle of 'enterprising' hawkers that has
grown up around it: anyone want to buy an American flag and
a little tin of ashes? Don't think so. The rest of the downtown
area was back on its feet fairly quickly, and there's no real reason
you shouldn't get down there and go about your honest tourist
business.

眞善美化妆品總匯

SHISE
CHAIN S

LISA
COSMETICS

愛 Ai·HOA 華
SUPERMARKET

第一牙

化妆品

愛華起

Downtown, Chinatown

Around Town

New York is a totally different town depending on which area you choose to visit, going from scuzzy beyond belief to rinkier and dinkier than anywhere else in the known universe. I've split the town into pretty generally recognised areas, some of which are tourist districts with not much that is specifically gay (the Financial District), some of which are gay with no real reason for the general tourist to go there (Hell's Kitchen in Midtown). If you're pushed for time, drop the whole Harlem/Brooklyn thing: no matter how hip everyone wants them to be, they're still a very long way from giving the likes of SoHo and Midtown a run for their money.

Downtown, Chinatown and Little Italy

The Downtown area is a big one, so wear comfy shoes. It's a mixture of financial and touristy, so you're not going to see much in the way of real New York life – unless you count the swarm of office workers power-walking to their buildings at rush hour, that is. The vibe changes from the laid-back strollers and skaters in Battery Park to the ridiculously stressed-out of the New York Financial District. But if you can't quite decide what you're in the mood for, this is a great day out as there are bridges to cross, towers to scale, ferries to take and shops to shop in. Hop on the subway down to Bowling Green – New York's oldest bit of greenery and a great place to start – and remember that if you're going to do the Statue of Liberty, there goes most of your day.

To add Lower East Side, Chinatown and Little Italy would make a hellish day of it, but they're in the general vicinity.

A DAY OUT

One of the greatest free things you can do in Manhattan is take the Staten Island Ferry, the one mentioned in Joni Mitchell's *Song for Sharon* from the

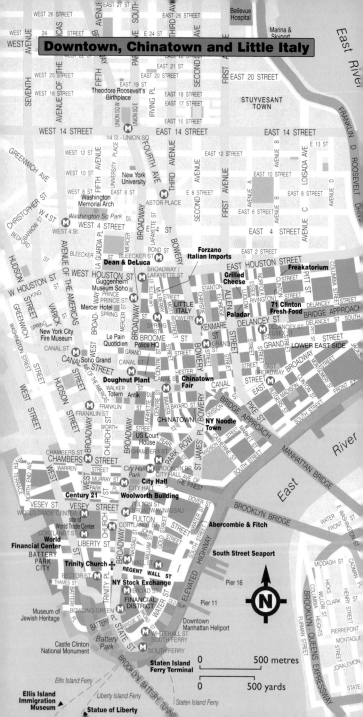

Hejira album and featured in the film *Working Girl*. It's not like you're going to want to get off at Staten Island or anything, but the trip will take you as near to the Statue of Liberty as you really need to go. If you bag yourself a space at the back of the ferry – it doesn't turn round at the other end, so stay put when you arrive – you'll get some great shots of your travelling companions against the backdrop of the skyscrapers of the Financial District. Go to the Staten Island Ferry Terminal and up the ramp and mill around until you hear the scrape of the ferry on the dock outside.

If you're determined to visit the Statue of Liberty and the Ellis Island Museum (*see Stepping Out, p. 16*), the ferry leaves from a stop to the right of the Ferry Terminal if you have your back to the city. Walk over there anyway and you'll find Battery Park and Battery Park City, which has been completely redone and is now a great little waterside walk. Just follow it round, dodging the rollerbladers, and you'll come to the huge atrium at the World Financial Center. The walk from Battery Park City across to Brooklyn Bridge is long, but there are plenty of things to see along the way. There's the Woolworth Building, which used to be a big deal in the early days of skyscrapers, when it was all about who could get highest fastest, and City Hall, which has been the mayor's residence since the early 1800s. There's nothing much to do here except get married and check out the renovated City Hall Park. From there, you've got two options. Either you can go straight to the sweeping span of the Brooklyn Bridge, or you can head back downtown to check out the financial district.

Statues in Battery Park

AROUND TOWN

Sign on Stock Exchange wall

On your way to Wall Street, dive into Century 21 (*see Shopping, p. 71*), an enormous 16-department store that sells off cut-price designer goodies and have a look around the quaint Trinity Church. You can actually go in the New York Stock Exchange at 20 Broad Street and look down on the crazy people doing their buying and selling, while in Wall Street itself you'll find the highly recognisable Regent Wall Street, now a huge hotel.

If you took the other route towards Brooklyn Bridge, take that legendary journey across it on the pedestrian walkway and be prepared to use half your film stock (*see Stepping Out, p. 13*). The South Street Seaport area is also a great place to get shots of the bridge and of the tall ships moored there. The area is a real tourist trap full of pubs and seafood restaurants. One of its major attractions is the only Abercrombie and Fitch store in Manhattan – the place to go for all your souvenir T-shirt requirements (*see All Shopped Out, p. 67*).

Yes, you've done plenty already so you might want to leave Chinatown, Little Italy and the Lower East Side to another day. You might even want to skip it altogether, which would be no great crime as these are areas that may be famous from the cinema, but really don't have much for the tourist unless it's total immersion in New York you're after. For that, the Lower East Side is the place. It's where Madonna shacked up when she first arrived in the city, and though it's grungy, it's not frighteningly so. You could kick off with a truly out-of-this-world organic doughnut from the Donut Plant at 379 Grand Street. It's just a tiny counter and single seat with coffee coming out of a flask so don't expect luxury, but those doughnuts are pretty unbeatable. (You can also get them at Dean & DeLuca if you don't want the full Lower East Side experience – *see p. 69*.)

From here, wander northwards, across Delancey Street and explore the neighbourhood around Ludlow, Essex and Norfolk. This area may be a bit dirty but it has lots of heart and plenty of Spanish music pouring out of the various shops. Put your head in at the Freakatorium at 57 Clinton Street, a brilliant and bizarre shop-cum-freak show where you can peruse exhibits linked to the Elephant Man and other less famous sideshow folk. Here you can buy excellent T-shirts and postcards and even get hold of a shrunken head for a mere $20 (... don't think they're real).

There are some cool places to drop in for food, like Grilled Cheese at 168 Ludlow Street, a tiny, funky bare-brick affair with laid-back staff and a few raggedy tables and chairs, and Cuban restaurant Paladar at 161 Ludlow Street, with its kitsch interior and deliciously authentic food. In fact, this whole area has become an after-dark favourite with diners, with restaurants like 71 Clinton Fresh Food (*see Eating Out p. 84*) and discerning locals who wouldn't usually be seen dead in this part of town.

Southwest of Lower East Side you are confronted with a whole new ethnic flavour as you hit Chinatown. See it if you must but, be warned, it's filthy, noisy, busy and – especially on a warm day – stinks to high heaven. Besides which, there's not a whole lot for the tourist to do unless you're in the market for some cheap embroidered slippers or want a flattened duck for lunch. And beware the 'bargains' and fake designer goods – you really will get what you pay for. You can walk along Canal Street and see the food stalls, stop off at one of the numerous restaurants on Mott Street for a cheap meal or waste some money in the almost unbearable Chinatown Fair amusement arcade. To the west of Chinatown is the Bowery, once a meeting place for tramps, which pretty much says it all.

If you want to have some Chinese while you're down here, the award-winning New York Noodle Town, an unglamorous but delicious noodle bar on the Bowery, is an ideal place for some chow.

As for Little Italy, the area to the north of Chinatown, it may be famous from all those *Godfather* films, but there's very little to do here except wander the streets, check out the Italian cafés on Mulberry Street or maybe pick up a Virgin Mary at Forzano Italian Imports at 128 Mulberry Street.

Manhattan's buildings jostle for space

☕ Out to Lunch

While there is no shortage of sandwich bars to feed the workers and tourist restaurants, the Downtown area is actually a bit of a tricky one for the discerning, unless you want to bunk into Tribeca next door. If you do the Lower East Side or Chinatown thing, look at the restaurants already mentioned.

Any filling you like

OUTLINES

BATTERY PARK
ⓘ Between State and Whitehall Streets and Battery Place
Ⓜ Subway 1, 9 to South Ferry; 4, 5 to Bowling Green

This green, statue-filled area at the tip of Manhattan has breezy views across to Ellis Island and the Statue of Liberty. This is where thousands of hopeful immigrants first set foot on the 'land of the free'.

BATTERY PARK CITY
ⓘ Between West Street and the Hudson River, Battery Park and Chambers Street
www.batteryparkcity.org

Thirty acres of open space stretching up the south-western tip of Manhattan with a great view across the river, familiar benches to slouch on and more than enough rollerbladers.

CITY HALL
ⓘ City Hall Park, between Broadway and Park Row and Chambers Street
Ⓜ Subway J, M, Z to Chambers Street; 2, 3 to Park Place; 4, 5, 6 to Brooklyn Bridge-City Hall

It's from this 1812 building that the mayor runs the city. There are some famous stairs where you've seen people give press conferences and get confetti thrown on them, and it's set in a newly refurbished park.

New York Stock Exchange

DOWNTOWN, CHINATOWN AND LITTLE ITALY

ELLIS ISLAND IMMIGRATION MUSEUM

212-363-3200
Subway N, R to Whitehall Street; 1, 9 to South Ferry; 4, 5 to Bowling Green. Ferry from Gangway 4 or 5 in Battery Park. Ferry times vary according to time of year. First ferry: 8.30am in summer, 9am rest of year. Last ferry: 6.45pm in summer, 6.30pm rest of year. Tickets are sold until 3.30pm.

You reach Ellis Island on the way back from the Statue of Liberty. It's huge and haunting. Check out the audio tour and visit the website before you go to find out if you have family who passed through this gateway to America.

NEW YORK STOCK EXCHANGE

20 Broad Street at Wall Street
212-656-5165
www.nyse.com
Mon–Fri 8.45am–4.30pm
Subway J, M, Z to Broad Street; 2, 3, 4, 5 to Wall Street
Admission free

Go to the gallery and watch the stockbrokers doing their crazy thing.

SOUTH STREET SEAPORT

Water Street to East River
Subway: A, C, J, M, Z, 2, 3, 4, 5 to Fulton Street–Broadway Nassau

There's not much to do here but look at the replicas of tall ships and the touristy restaurants and shops.

STATUE OF LIBERTY

(see Ellis Island, above, for ferry times)

Remember that tickets to the crown are limited during peak season to the first ferry.

TRINITY CHURCH

74 Trinity Place Broadway at Wall Street
212-602-0800
www.trinitywallstreet.org
Mon–Fri 9am–11.45am and 1pm–3.45pm; Sat 10am–3.45pm; Sun 1pm–3.45pm

Subway N, R to Rector Street
Admission free

A cute little church with tours every day from 2pm, and a museum.

WALL STREET

Subway 2, 3, 4, 5 to Wall Street; J, M, Z to Broad Street

Come at 8.30am and see those worker ants going mad.

WOOLWORTH BUILDING

233 Broadway between Park Place and Barclay Street
Office hours
Subway N, R to City Hall; 2, 3 to Park Place
Admission free

A fine example of an early 20th-century highrise building before the really big skyscrapers took over.

Trinity Church

SoHo is a shopper's paradise

SoHo and Tribeca

SoHo is the main shopping area for artsy items from clothes and interiors to lotions and lemon tarts made from an ancient recipe. As an area, it has a vibe that is one of the coolest in the whole of New York City, and the weekend's a great time to have a look. Despite it being hellishly busy, you get to see Manhattan resting and playing, and spending their wages on leisurely brunches and expensive clothing until well into the evening (the shops stay open till 7 or 8pm). Make at least a day of it, and rest between purchases in one of the many cafés or bars, whether it's to leisurely sip on one of the many varieties of coffees or to knock back a Cosmopolitan cocktail. And make sure you leave Tribeca till the night-time, when its hot bars and expensive restaurants wake up the area.

A DAY OUT

Make your way by subway to Canal Street and start your day off the right way with breakfast at Le Pain Quotidien at 100 Grand Street (*see Eating Out, p. 82*) and then get ready to shop. You'll need a shot of caffeine at the very least to keep you going all day.

You could spend your whole time in New York walking up and down the grid of streets between Canal in the south and Houston in the north – SoHo actually stands for South of Houston – taking in the loft architecture, the cast-iron frame buildings, the cinematic fire escapes and boutiques like Stussy and APC.

Don't forget Moss, up where Greene meets Houston, for one of the best interior design shops in town and, if you time it right, you could be in the perfect place for a pre-lunch cocktail at the bar in the swanky Mercer Hotel.

Walk east to Broadway and you'll find not only a huge new Prada shop but also the Guggenheim Museum's SoHo branch. You have to go up in a lift, and never mind what the

Hold it

SoHo and Tribeca

WASHINGTON SQ NORTH

Washington Memorial Arch
Washington Sq Park

WEST HOUSTON STREET

Once Upon A Tart

Stussy

Moss

New Museum of Contemporary Art

Guggenheim Museum SoHo

Fanelli

APC

Banana Republic

The Mercer Hotel

Prada

Canal Jeans

Haughwout Building

New York City Fire Museum

SOHO

BROOME STREET

GRAND STREET

Soho Grand

Doughnut Plant

Le Pain Quotidien

Museum of Photography

HOWARD

Screening Room

CANAL STREET

LISPENARD STREET

WALKER STREET

WHITE

Totem

Antik

FRANKLIN

LEONARD STREET

TRIBECA

WORTH STREET

THOMAS STREET

DUANE STREET

Washington Market Park

READE ST

CHAMBERS STREET

CHAMBERS ST

WARREN STREET

MURRAY STREET

PARK

CITY HALL

City Hall Park

Woolworth Building

Hudson River

North Park

0   200 metres

0   200 yards

N

exhibition is (it's free anyway), the space is brilliant: a huge loft with cast-iron pillars, some of them gilded.

Broadway at this level is a shopper's paradise of a different kind to SoHo. Apart from the brilliant Dean & DeLuca delicatessen (*see p. 69*) across the road from the Guggenheim, this area is made for the bargain-hunter. The whole of this section of Broadway is given over to cut-price clothes shops like Banana Republic, Armani Exchange and Club Monaco and vast migraine-inducing emporia like Canal Jeans.

Beyond Broadway you'll find more interesting stores, albeit more spaced out. There's Keith Haring's brilliant little Pop Shop (*see p. 70*) filled with items covered in the little graffiti dogs and babies that made his name and the gorgeous Creed, to name just a couple of your many options here.

Heading back south-east, you'll come to Tribeca, or the Triangle Below Canal Street. Although this is one of the coolest areas in New York, and one with ample bars and restaurants to feed and water its hip inhabitants, there isn't necessarily that much for the visitor to make a bee-line for. If you're up for a little furniture shopping – though how you'll ever get it home is anyone's guess – the area around Franklin Street is for you. There you'll find the cutting-edge Totem (or The Objects That Evoke Meaning) and Antik, selling modern classics. Come back after dark for the full effect.

Keith Haring's art at the Pop Shop

☕ Out to Lunch

Freshly brewed

In SoHo, you are truly spoilt for lunch options. If you don't want to take too much time out from your shopping, **Once Upon A Tart** is ideal. Choose a nice home-baked savoury tart and a salad from the counter, grab a juice and perch at one of the ten crammed-in tables for a quarter of an hour. Actually, you probably won't be able to resist a rock cake and a coffee to follow, so you might not be as quick as you'd planned. Alternatively, for an equally old-school experience, you could pop into **Fanelli's** for a quick and inexpensive spaghetti or burger. Fanelli's is ancient, a little on the grungy side, but very real and very easy. Or you could just grab a delicious soup from the attached kiosk and eat it on the street.

OUTLINES

GUGGENHEIM MUSEUM SOHO

🆔 575 Broadway at Prince Street

📞 212-423-3500

www.guggenheim.org

🕐 Thu–Mon 11am–6pm; Tues and Wed closed

Ⓜ Subway N, R to Prince Street, 6 to Spring Street or B, D, F, Q to Broadway-Lafayette 💲 $5

A brilliant little museum stop in the middle of all that shopping, the Guggenheim Museum in SoHo is a great example of the typical neighbourhood cast-iron architecture. It is also currently showing Andy Warhol's excellent *Last Supper* series on a semi-permanent basis.

NEW MUSEUM OF CONTEMPORARY ART

🆔 583 Broadway between Houston and Prince Street

📞 212-219-1222

www.newmuseum.org

Ⓜ Subway 6 to Spring or Bleecker St, N, R to Prince St, A, C, E to Spring St or B,

D, F, Q to Broadway
Lafayette
 Tues–Sun noon–6pm
(Thu 8pm); closed Mon
$6

If you're turned on by the avant-garde, keep an eye on exhibitions at this art space near the SoHo Guggenheim. Since it opened in 1977, it's made a name for itself for putting on controversial exhibitions and having a fine bookstore with readings, performances and the odd book signing. There are also some great gifts.

Read all about it

If you want to take a New York-flavoured book with you, there really is no shortage of material, from Jay McInerny's yuppie-loser novel *Bright Lights, Big City*, to Brett Easton Ellis's murderously funny *American Psycho,* both with plenty of bar and club name-checks. Jennifer Belle's hysterical *Going Down*, about a girl who drifts gaily into prostitution, is set all over town, while James St James's gripping and hilarious *Disco Bloodbath* tells the true story of how New York's club scene spiralled into drug-induced madness and ended in grisly murder. Candace Bushnell's *Sex and the City* is much nastier than the TV show, but just as compelling, while Felice Picano's big old holiday novel *Like People in History* has some great late 1970s Fire Island scenes featuring nightspots that are still there.

Guggenheim Museum SoHo

Strumming in Washington Square

Greenwich Village

The Village is a huge, amorphous area that, after the easy-to-know-where-you-are grid system of most of Manhattan, can seem like a real maze. And, considering it has been a byword for alternative living and counter-culture for close on 40 years, it can also be a bit of a disappointment for lovers of cool, now that most of the cool has moved on to SoHo or Chelsea, leaving behind quite a lot of hippy tat. It is worth a visit for the historical Washington Square area and for speed-flicking through CDs and vinyl in some of the area's brilliant record stores. As for the area around Christopher Street, once the undisputed centre of the gay universe (well, the Village People were named after this place!), it's still pretty but now a bit on the sad side with not much more than a couple of fairly down-at-heel bars and sex shops to its name.

A DAY OUT

Hop on subway 1 or 9 to Christopher Street-Sheridan Square and you'll find yourself in the leafy streets of Greenwich Village. You can head west and check out the piers that used to be Manhattan cruising central (and that once played host to the lamented yet most hair-raising gay event in New York, Wigstock) or you can have a wander along Christopher Street, taking in the oldest gay bookshop in the world, the Oscar Wilde Memorial Bookshop at number 15. Now that A Different Light, previously the main gay bookshop, has closed down, this is pretty much the only one, so make the most of it and the other little boutiques well worth browsing around before you head east to Washington Square.

You might want to take a little detour north to Balducci's (424 Sixth Avenue at 9th Street), an amazing food emporium selling global goodies. The coffee here is amazing and you should take a bag back to remind yourself of the great cups of 'kwarfee' you'll be served in NYC.

In Washington Square you can hang out on the grass in the knowledge that the likes of Bob Dylan and Robert Mapplethorpe have been there before you. You'll recognise the Arc de Triomphe thing (the Washington Square Arch – a tribute to George Washington) and can just flake around with the students resting between lectures – most of this area is university-related – as well as the skate kids making use of the open space. The area's hippie past is still occasionally visible, and street musicians make the most of passing locals and tourists, as do the funny-coloured squirrels.

If records and CDs are your thing, head south to Bleecker Street for some real finds. The best of the lot is Bleecker Street Records at number 39. A huge paradise for anyone who likes flicking through rows of CDs,

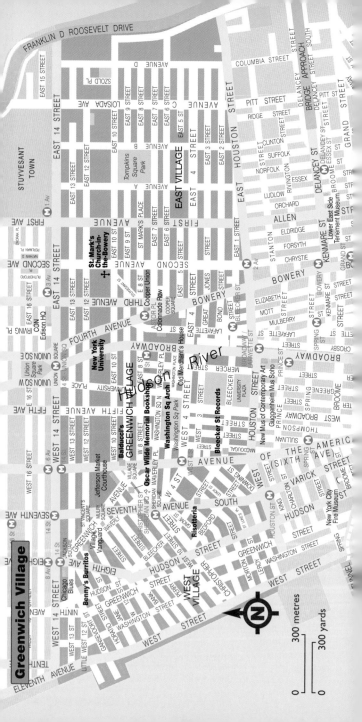

it has treasures in the form of bootlegs and rare editions you really won't find anywhere else.

Heading east, you'll notice a definite change in vibe. The East Village, an extension of the Lower East Side, has a history of attracting everyone from punks to drug dealers to the homeless, who once colonised the whole of Tompkins Square Park, and who, even though they've been evicted, still clearly have a soft spot for it.

St Mark's Place

On your way to Tompkins Square Park (it really wouldn't hurt to give it a miss, though), you go along St Mark's Place, a real find if you're in the market for some retro vinyl, a punk T-shirt and maybe a tattoo. If you've come to NYC for glamour, give the whole area a miss, even though in the evening the real East Village with its bars and restaurants of all descriptions comes alive.

 # Out to Lunch

Queues often form in the evenings for **Benny's Burritos**. Don't be expecting linen napkins and your finest crystal as it's kitsch 1960s styling and formica surfaces all the way. Go at lunch time and fill up on fajitas, burritos and fresh guacamole, all washed down with a margarita. Great fresh food with bargain basement prices.

Alternatively, be dazzled by the choice of risottos over at the **Risotteria** on Bleecker Street, a steel and wood affair where you order at the counter and sit back and wait for the huge salads and creamy risottos to arrive (*see Eating Out, p. 87*).

Benny's Burritos

AROUND TOWN

OUTLINES

CHURCH OF ST MARK'S-IN-THE-BOWERY

ℹ 131 East 10th Street at Second Avenue

✆ 212-674-6377

www.saintmarkschurch.org

Ⓜ Subway 6 to Astor Place

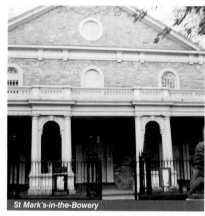
St Mark's-in-the-Bowery

In the middle of the St Mark's Historic District, St Mark's-in-the-Bowery is New York's second-oldest church dating back to 1799. Check out the graveyard and you might come across the memorial plaque for gay poet W. H. Auden, who was a local.

TOMPKINS SQUARE PARK

ℹ Between East 7th and 10th Streets and Avenues A and B

Ⓜ Subway 6 to Astor Place

Once something of a no-go area because of the homeless people, squatters and drug dealers who made it their own, Tompkins Square Park is a nice enough green respite from the rather gritty East Village surroundings. However, it is still a little tatty for some tastes.

WASHINGTON SQUARE PARK

ℹ Between 4th Street and Waverley Place, University Place and MacDougal Street

Ⓜ Subway A, C, E, B, D, F, Q to W 4th Street

Once a pretty dodgy place filled with roughs and drug dealers, Washington Square Park is now somewhere to flop down on the grass (okay, it's not exactly lush, but it'll do), laze by the fountain and watch the students going about their business. Surrounded by buildings, which, by American standards are fairly historic. The Washington Square Arch, which, like the square, is named after George Washington, was built in 1812.

Cooling off in Washington Square

Leafy Village intersection

The striking Flatiron Building

Chelsea

Chelsea is Boyztown NYC, the area gay men started moving to when there was no more room in the Village. Although there is an historic side to it, it is basically somewhere to cruise, have lunch, buy some gay nonsense and maybe go to the gym. Mind you, west of the main drag on Eighth Avenue there's a new artsy atmosphere beginning to build as galleries and chic designers move in. Move to the east and the atmosphere changes from street and gay through to hip at Union Square, where the fashion people brunch. And go further east and you'll find where they live, in quiet, residential Gramercy Park. But for our purposes, it's all about Chelsea and the newly revitalised meatpacking district, now an ultra-chic area filled with some of the hippest restaurants and clubs in town.

A DAY OUT

Jump the 1 or 9 subways down to 18th Street and start your Chelsea morning with brunch at Food Bar (*see p. 81*). As you leave, you'll find you are surrounded by gay retail outlets: clothes stores, art shops, places full of knick-knacks and porn videos and pharmacies specialising in HIV treatment; they're all side by side along this stretch of Eighth Avenue. There's a gym and a grooming station and... well, you get the picture. Once you've checked out the shops, get a coffee in The Big Cup, a bohemian café that's something of a Chelsea institution (*see p. 87*).

If you wander over to the west of Chelsea you can check out the ultra-funky Dia Center for the Arts (the tiles are dizzying, but they won't let you take pictures) and the little private galleries that are sprouting up along 22nd Street. While you're there, put your head into the brilliant new Comme des Garçons shop. The clothes are terrible, but the interior is amazing. Right over by the Hudson, across the West Side Freeway, you'll find the huge and quite depressing sports centre called Chelsea Piers. And on your way back east, stop off at Chelsea Market, which has a great food section well worth having a look at.

Moving back east, up on busy 23rd Street you'll pass the infamous Chelsea Hotel where Sid killed Nancy and where Burroughs, Ginsberg and the gang hung out. Have a look around the gallery-like lobby and see where Warhol filmed his early classic *Chelsea Girls*.

Carry on along the street as far as Broadway and you'll come to the fantastic Flatiron Building, a 100-year-old oddity of an edifice so pointy you wonder what those rooms must look like inside. From here you can wander down Broadway to Union Square, where you'll find hip cafés and restaurants rubbing up against Virgin Megastores.

There's not much point in wandering much further east as all you'll find is Gramercy Park, which you can't get into as it's for residents only. The houses are nice, but there's not much to do.

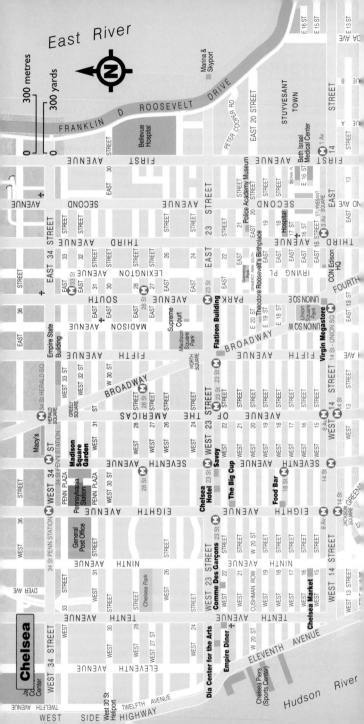

Out to Lunch

Art Deco diner

Chelsea's **Empire Diner** is the place to eat in the neighbourhood. After all, Bette Davis declared it her favourite diner. A gleamingly restored 1929 Art Deco diner that attracts a lively crowd of trendy customers pretty much around the clock. Come here for a lunchtime burger or a midnight feast.

OUTLINES

CHELSEA MARKET

75 Ninth Avenue between 15th and 16th Streets | Subway A, C, E to 14th Street or L to 8th Avenue

Mon–Sat 8am–7pm, Sun 10am–6pm

Shop for food instead of clothing for a change.

EMPIRE DINER

210 10th Avenue

212-243-2736

Daily 24 hours

A classic, yet contemporary New York institution. Popular with young clubbers both before and after a big night out. (*See also Eating Out, p. 88*)

Shopping for bargains around Chelsea

Times Square – just a jump to the left . . .

Midtown

This is where most of Manhattan spends its nine to five, but just because offices dominate the massive Midtown area, it doesn't make it in any way dull. The skyscrapers are sexy, the shops sometimes even sexier. If you've come to New York to shop, then you're easily going to need more than one day in the Midtown area. Bordered by Central Park in the north and Chelsea in the south, you've also got iconic landmarks such as the Empire State Building (*see p. 14*) and the Chrysler Building and the burgeoning new gay area of Hell's Kitchen over on the West Side (it's where *West Side Story* was set, but it's cleaned up its act quite remarkably since then). With its skyscrapers and swanky stores and the old-school Manhattan of Hell's Kitchen, Midtown is pretty much what you think of when you think of New York.

A DAY OUT

All roads – well, subways N, R, S, 1, 2, 3, 7, 9 – lead to 42nd Street–Times Square. If neon and crowds are your thing this is a total must, but apart from a huge Gap store, a massive Virgin Megastore and the MTV studios, there's not really much else going on, though the eight-storey video screen of the Nasdaq Market Site is truly awe-inspiring.

Times Square is actually a triangle thanks to Broadway, the 'Great White Way', the street that cuts diagonally across the verticals and horizontals of Midtown before it falls in line with the Avenues at 8th Street. It's one of the most famous streets in the world, and you may wonder why. Yes, there are the huge theatres showing musicals and your Gaps and record stores, but it's not exactly mind-blowing.

Walk south and you'll come to Macy's (*see p. 74*), which occupies an entire city block and calls itself the biggest department store in the world, though size is pretty much all it has to recommend it.

You'll have heard of 42nd Street from the musical. A haunt of gypsies, tramps and thieves until Mayor Giuliani came down heavy in the 1990s, it is recovering but is really only interesting if you want to check out Madame Tussaud's or fancy browsing the theatres that made the street famous. If you do venture along 42nd Street from Broadway, by the time you get to Eighth Avenue, famous for its sex shops, you'll probably have had enough.

With the grungy Port Authority Bus Terminal on one side and cheesy, sleazy sex shops with those same drug dealers working their sidewalks (albeit more subtly), there's no real reason to come this far over except to visit the up-and-coming new district of Hell's Kitchen, the scary-sounding area around Ninth Avenue that is bustling with cool restaurants and gay bars. There are many original 19th-century Manhattan storefronts still to be

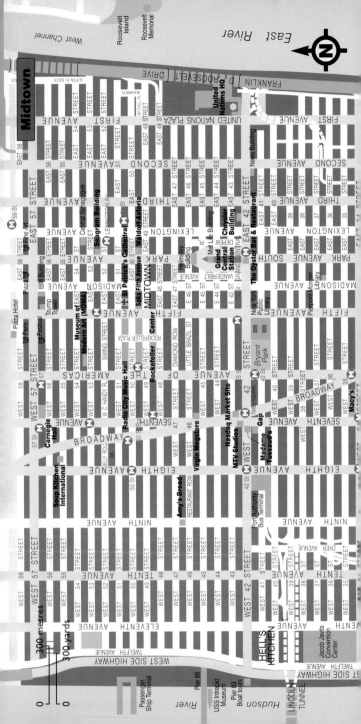

seen, and even though it's not an area with anything specific to check out, except the bars, it is worth wandering up a couple of streets just to take in the atmosphere. Amy's Bread on Ninth Avenue is a brilliant baker's turning out a dazzling array of breads and pastries. There are a few cheeky tables up the back so you can sit down to enjoy a delicious original apple doughnut.

Heading back East, you come to Fifth Avenue with the very sexy Saks Fifth Avenue department store and pretty much every clothing store you could wish for from H&M to Gucci. There is also the beautifully Deco Rockefeller Center, with its famous ice rink, and MoMA, on 52nd Street, currently undergoing a billion-dollar refurbishment (*see p. 15*).

Standing out a mile amidst the towers of Fifth Avenue is St Patrick's Cathedral, a traditional Gothic church whose spire struggles to match the surrounding skyscrapers. And while you're walking down Fifth, cast your eye along 50th Street in the direction of Sixth Avenue and you'll see the famous red neon of Radio City Music Hall, a venue that plays host to everything from the Christmas Rockettes dancers to Oasis (*see Playing Around Town, p. 109*).

Midtown is by far the best neighbourhood for skyscraper-spotting. Zigzag between the Corbusier-influenced United Nations Headquarters building over on First Avenue in the east and back west via the high-Deco Chrysler, to the beautiful Mies van der Rohe Seagram Building on Park Avenue, and don't forget the Empire State Building (*see Stepping Out, p. 14*).

Take the E Train

Out to Lunch

For something a little bit special, head to the beautifully restored Grand Central Terminal on 42nd Street. Get yourself to the **Oyster Bar and Restaurant** after the lunchtime rush, grab a stool by the bar and tuck into some of the city's best oysters and seafood – if you're going really mad, get them to crack open a bottle of champagne too. Noisy and very Manhattan, but also incredibly romantic, it's the perfect shopping break in Midtown. **Soup Kitchen International** (259A West 55th Street) is a good cheap

Grand Central seafood

option. Expect rude staff (*Seinfeld's* 'Soup Nazi' episode was based on this place) and absolutely amazing varieties of soup dishes.

OUTLINES

CHRYSLER BUILDING

ℹ️ 405 Lexington Avenue at 42nd Street

Ⓜ️ Subway S, 4, 5, 6, 7 to 42nd Street-Grand Central

This beautiful pointy skyscraper with a metal nib that glints in the sun was built in 1930 and is still one of the prettier buildings in NYC. Step inside and take in the Art Deco lobby and its exquisite lift doors.

EMPIRE STATE BUILDING

ℹ️ 34th Street-Herald Square

📞 212-736-3100
www.esbnyc.com

🕐 9.30am–11.30pm

Ⓜ️ Subway B, D, F, Q, N, R to 34th Street

💲 $7, cash only

This mighty monolith is one of the city's key attractions (*see p. 14*).

GRAND CENTRAL STATION

ℹ️ 42nd to 44th Streets between Vanderbilt and Lexington Avenues

Ⓜ️ Subway S, 4, 5, 6, 7 to 42nd Street-Grand Central

So much more than just a station, the terminal has been lovingly restored (*see also p. 14*).

MUSEUM OF MODERN ART (MOMA)

ℹ️ 11 West 53rd Street

One of the world's largest collections of modern art. Moving to Queens (*see p. 15*), but due back here in 2004.

NASDAQ MARKET SITE

ℹ️ 4 Times Square Broadway at 43rd Street

📞 877-627-3271

Ⓜ️ Subway 1, 2, 3, 9, N, R, S, to 42nd Street-Times Square (not 7)

An amazing building-as-TV-screen affair, this is the stock market for new media.

RADIO CITY MUSIC HALL

🛈 6th Avenue at 50th Street

🚇 Subway B, D, F, Q to 47th-50th Street-Rockefeller Center.

See page 109.

ROCKEFELLER CENTER

🛈 48th to 51st Street between 5th and 6th Avenues | 🚇 Subway B, D, F, Q to 47–50th Streets-Rockefeller Center

See page 15.

ST PATRICK'S CATHEDRAL

🛈 5th Avenue between 50th and 51st Streets

📞 212-753-2261

🕙 Sun–Fri 7am–8.45pm; Sat 8am–8.45pm.

Ring for times of Cathedral tours.

🚇 Subway B, D, F, Q to 47–50th Streets-Rockefeller Center or E, F to Fifth Avenue

SEAGRAM BUILDING

🛈 375 Park Avenue between 52nd and 53rd Streets.

🚇 Subway E, F to Lexington Avenue or 6 to 51st Street.

Stand and stare at this gorgeous piece by Mies van der Rohe.

TIMES SQUARE

🛈 42nd Street at Broadway | 🚇 Subway N, R, S, 1, 2, 3, 7, 9 to Times Square-42nd Street

See page 16.

UNITED NATIONS HEADQUARTERS

🛈 1st Avenue at 46th Street | 📞 212-963-7713

🚇 Subway S, 4, 5, 6, 7 to 42nd Street-Grand Central.

🕙 9.15am–4.45pm
Tours every half hour

💲 $7.50

A modernist master-piece inspired by the great Corbusier. The Peace Garden is also worth a look.

Times Square – the light show

The famous skyline viewed from the green of Central Park

Upper East Side

This is where the money lives in NYC. With designer stores packing Madison Avenue, the beautiful cultural institutions on Museum Mile, and the fantastic apartments lining the leafy edge of Central Park, this is where the ridiculously rich Manhattanites hang, making it, despite everything, a rather uninspiring neighbourhood.

If you don't want to do the museums, then you'll really only need a few hours to wander the mostly residential streets and check out the eccentric monied Upper East Side ladies trotting from one appointment to another. Unless you're shopping, that is. If you're shopping, put aside time and big money. And after a hard day's sidewalk stomping – or art ogling – head to the Metropolitan Museum of Art's rooftop bar at sunset for breathtaking views over Central Park and the city.

A DAY OUT

'Doing' the museums on Museum Mile in a single day is not only impossible but verging on the criminal. The National Academy of Design, the Jewish Museum, El Museo Del Barrio – you name it, it's here. If you are tight for time, stick to this selection.

Take subway 4, 5, 6 to 86th Street, walk over towards Central Park and up a couple of blocks to the Solomon R. Guggenheim Museum building, which is art in itself. Frank Lloyd Wright's spiralling rotunda always looks like it could do with a lick of paint, but makes for a great photo album shot from a distance. Check press like the *Village Voice* (*see p. 143*) for listings of current exhibitions.

Walk downtown five blocks and you'll get to the Metropolitan Museum of Art, one of the world's largest and most impressive museums, with a collection that spans 5,000 years from the prehistoric to the present. Highlights to head for are the Temple of Dendur, the Roof Gardens and the European collections.

From there, the Whitney Museum of American Art, famed for its controversial exhibitions, is six blocks down. This big brutal slab of a building is worth a visit in itself, as is Sarabeth's Restaurant at the Whitney, which on Sunday is packed with brunchers. If you want a light museum experience, do the Whitney – the Hopper collection is very New York – and work it round that brunch.

As you walk back downtown, make sure you stick to Madison Avenue. A major fashion house without a Madison Avenue address isn't worth its salt, and you'll find Calvin Klein's beautiful, minimal store by British architect John Pawson, Chloé, Diesel (but not cheaper than the UK), DKNY, Dolce & Gabbana and Prada. It's luxury all the way here, so don't

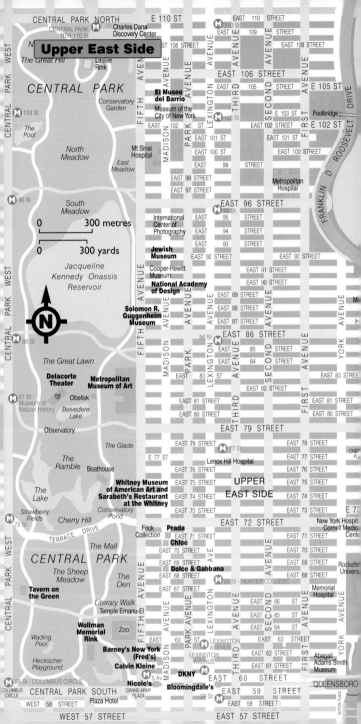

expect to find a bargain. The Italian fashion houses aren't actually any cheaper than in Europe – apart from their timepieces – but American favourites like designs from Donna Karan will be cheaper by sometimes up to 20%.

East Side fashion

As well as big-name designers, the Upper East Side also boasts two of New York's finest department stores. Barney's New York on Madison at 61st Street is something of an institution. It has a whole menswear store with eight floors of ultra-modern designs by the likes of McQueen, Helmut Lang and the Prada family, with lesser-known but no less cool designers on offer on the Co-Op floors.

Over on Lexington is Bloomingdale's, which, despite falling behind the times somewhat, has started to improve again over recent years. Definitely not the best store for contemporary fashions, it does however boast a great bag and sunglasses section, as well as some gorgeous home furnishings. There's also a massive, ridiculously camp 'Barbie Boutique' up on fifth. It's worth making a purchase so you can swing a Little Brown Bag like a true New Yorker.

Designer department store

Out to Lunch

Ready for lunch

The Upper East Side is all about your dollars, so you may as well eat in style. **Nicole's** at Nicole Farhi's swanky Madison Avenue store has gained accolades such as 'best in-store restaurant' and it certainly doesn't disappoint. With lush wooden flooring, and a sexy underlit marble refectory-style table running down one end of the restaurant, this place oozes glamour.

If you can't bear to drag yourself away from **Barney's**, then check out the store's very own eatery, Fred's. Busy, buzzy and hip, it serves everything from club sandwiches to lobster salad. **Bloomingdale's** cafeteria is a perfect place for a cheaper fill. Sandwiches, salads and free drink refills are served where the shop staff eat, so you know it's a bargain (*see p. 74*).

OUTLINES

METROPOLITAN MUSEUM OF ART

🛈 1000 5th Avenue, Central Park at 82nd Street

📞 212-535-7710

www.metmuseum.org

🕙 Sun, Tues–Thu 9:30am–5:30pm; Fri–Sat 9:30am–9:00pm; Mon closed

🚇 Subway 4, 5, 6 to 86th Street

💲 $10 suggested donation

This is probably the world's greatest col-lection of artworks, from ancient to modern and from Islamic through post-Impressionist European to the stellar Costume Institute. It is so huge that you really shouldn't venture in without an idea of what you want to see.

NATIONAL ACADEMY OF DESIGN

🛈 1083 5th Avenue at 89th Street

📞 212-369-4880

🕙 Wed, Thu, Sat, Sun noon–5pm; Fri 10am–6pm

🚇 Subway 4, 5, 6 to 86th Street

John Singer Sargent and Frank Lloyd Wright are just two of the American geniuses honoured in this strange fine art museum specialising in home-grown art from the last two centuries.

SOLOMON R. GUGGENHEIM MUSEUM

🛈 1071 5th Avenue at 89th Street

📞 212-423-3500

www.guggenheim.org

Whitney Museum of American Art

contains some international modern art masters like Picasso.

WHITNEY MUSEUM OF AMERICAN ART

ℹ️ 945 Madison Avenue at 75th Street

📞 212-570-3676

www.whitney.org

🕐 Mon closed; Tues–Wed 11am–6pm; Thu 1pm–9pm; Fri–Sun 11am–6pm

🚇 Subway 6 to 77th Street 💲 $10

🕐 Sun–Wed 9am–6pm; Fri–Sat 9am–8pm; Thu closed

🚇 Subway 4, 5, 6 to 86th Street

💲 $12

The helter-skelter of the building design is courtesy of America's greatest architect, Frank Lloyd Wright. The permanent collection

This brutal slab of a building specialises in American and cutting-edge art.

Solomon R. Guggenheim Museum

IMAGINE

It's easy if you try . . .

Upper West Side

The Upper West Side is grown-up New York. Don't think *West Side Story* – that was set in Hell's Kitchen down in the Midtown area. Do think media people (including Madonna), nice apartments, arts centres, huge bookshops and obviously, Central Park. In fact, it's such a media kind of place that Darren Star – the man behind *Sex and the City* – made a whole series called *Central Park West* based on New Yorkers who worked in magazines and lived in this area. In short, it's the kind of place you'd dream of moving to, away from the dirt of downtown and the tourists of Midtown, and with all the Pottery Barns and delis and, okay, smugness that you'd expect from an area with this kind of demographic.

A DAY OUT

Hop on the subway, trains A, C, B, D 1, 2, 3, 9, to 59 Street-Columbus Circle, and start your day in style with breakfast at the ultra-gorgeous Hudson Hotel on West 58th Street just off Broadway (*see p. 92*).

Start your wander just one block up at Columbus Circle, a roundabout-type affair on the south-western corner of Central Park.

One of the main draws of the Upper West Side, and something that contributes to the feel of the whole area, is the Lincoln Center. It's a collection of 1960s buildings, which are just starting to look great, that house the major New York music and dance organisations (*see also p. 107*). You can take a tour of the backstage areas and, if you're an opera buff, you shouldn't miss the Metropolitan Opera Shop, which is a real treasure trove (*see p. 76*).

Carrying on up Broadway, you come to some great shops, including what is probably the best record megastore in New York, Tower Records at 66th and Broadway. Straight across the road is probably the best Barnes & Noble bookshop in the city (*see p. 68*). A couple of blocks further up is the Sony Lincoln Square Cinema, a ridiculously big 12-screen multiplex with an IMAX screen thrown in for good measure (*see Playing Around Town, p. 109*).

Among the luxury residences on the Upper West Side worth seeking out are the Dakota (where John Lennon was assassinated and the film *Rosemary's Baby* was shot) and the Ansonia Hotel, which happens to be the former home of the Continental Baths, the gay hotspot where Bette Midler, Barry Manilow and Frankie Knuckles all started their careers performing for the gay towel crowd.

Move over to the west and you'll find Riverside Park, a formerly very swanky address with huge buildings to prove it. Run, cycle or just wander along looking at the houseboats in the 79th Street Boat Basin.

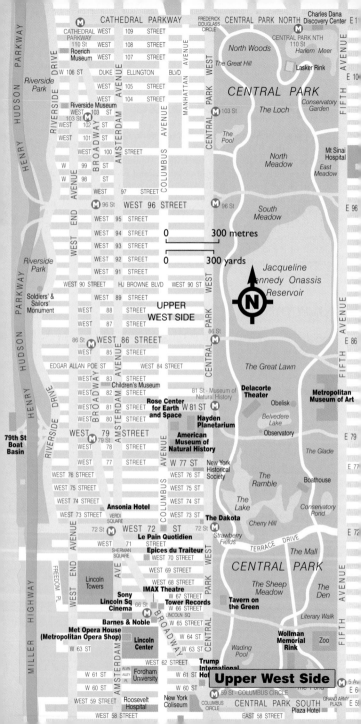

Upper West Side

The Lincoln Center from the Central Plaza

Overlooking Central Park is the highly respected American Museum of Natural History, the biggest in the world, with its dinosaurs and rainforests, and the Rose Center for Earth and Space, which includes the Hayden Planetarium.

In Central Park, whatever the season you can wander through the wooded Ramble, hire a boat, or jog at the Jacqueline Kennedy Onassis Reservoir.

If you can't decide what to eat, try Epices du Traiteur, a split-personality restaurant that can't quite decide whether it's French, Italian or North African. You can have anything from risotto and pasta to unpronounceable North African specialities. The staff have a bit of a reputation, but if you've had it up to here with 'Have a nice day', it can make a refreshing change. As Epices is only open in the evening, you might want to stop off at the Upper West Side branch of Le Pain Quotidien for a soup, sandwich or salad (see p. 82).

OUTLINES

AMERICAN MUSEUM OF NATURAL HISTORY
Central Park West at 79th Street
212-769-5000
www.amnh.org
Sun–Thu 10am–5.45pm; Fri–Sat 10am–8.45pm
Subway B, C to 81st Street

ANSONIA HOTEL
2109 Broadway between 73rd and 74th Streets
212-724-2600

Subway 1, 2, 3, 9 to 72nd Street

THE DAKOTA
72nd Street at Central Park West
Subway B, C to 72nd Street

Not open to the public.

DELACORTE THEATER
Central Park, enter the park at Central Park West at 81st Street
212-539-8750
www.publictheater.org
Subway B, C to 81st Street

LINCOLN CENTER
65th Street at Columbus Avenue
212-875-5400
www.lincolncenter.org
Subway 1, 9 to 66th Street-Lincoln Center

ROSE CENTER FOR EARTH AND SPACE, INCLUDING THE HAYDEN PLANETARIUM
West 81st Street at Central Park West
212-769-5900
Subway B, C to 81st Street

At the Museum of Natural History.

Legendary venue of black music

Harlem

It's hard to come to Harlem and not feel awkward about using other people's poverty as a tourist attraction. Although the area is obviously steeped in African-American history – jazz, hip hop, vogueing and black activism all have their roots here – it is still pretty grungy, even with recent government funding and the sharp drop in crime that's been felt all over New York City. Although Harlem, or parts of it, may well be safer than at anytime since the heyday of the 1920s, when rich whites would come on down for some jazz and liquor, tourists – especially white ones – don't exactly fit right in.

A DAY OUT

Take subway A, B, C, D, 2, 3 to 125th Street, which is Harlem central, and pay some dues to the rather sad-looking Apollo Theater where anyone who's anyone in black music (even some white folks) have shaken their booty over the years. It's on 125th Street that you'll see where most of the new money that has been invested in this area.

If you're an architecture buff, Harlem has some of the best brownstones in Manhattan (some of them going for millions now the area's on the up). It's really a question of wandering around, though there is a tradition of residents opening their houses to visitors one week in spring. Call 212-360-4241 for more on that. You can also take a look at Marcus Garvey Park or hop a little south to Morningside Heights, where university students from Columbia fill the cafés.

The Hamilton Heights Historic District has some great turn-of-the-century architecture and former famous residents like Duke Ellington and Count Basie. The only thing is, there's actually not that much to do.

Going uptown, you get to Washington Heights, which, like most of Manhattan's outer reaches, has seen an increase in residents as the property prices on the main section of the island have spiralled uncontrollably. The island is quite narrow here, flanked by Harlem and the Hudson River, and the further up you go the more you'll get the flavour (or aftertaste) of the city's original forest at Inwood Hill Park near 214th Street, the last refuge of Native Americans before they were completely driven from Manhattan.

Worth seeing if you feel the need to travel this far north is the historic Morris-Jumel Mansion, with its George Washington connections and palladian front. But the real must-see when you're up here is the Cloisters in Fort Tryon Park. A branch of the Metropolitan Museum, it's beautifully located in 50-odd acres of woods overlooking the Hudson River. The building is a recreation of a monastery; inside you'll find the Met's medieval collection including tapestries and sculptures.

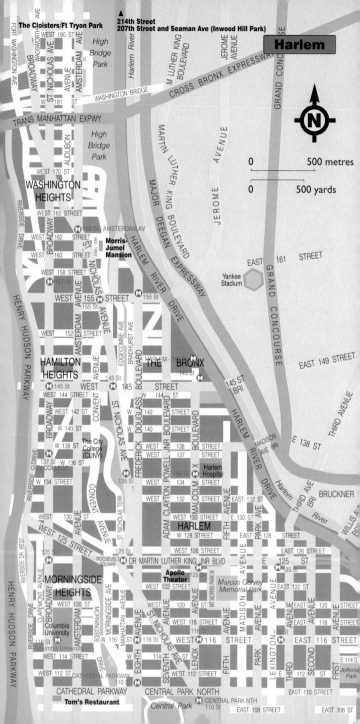

If you're a *Seinfeld* fan, you won't want to miss Tom's Restaurant, where the gang would often berate each other over brunch. The food is pretty standard diner nosh, but it is open 24 hours at weekends (see below).

OUTLINES

APOLLO THEATER

ℹ 125th Street between 7th and 8th Avenues

Ⓜ Subway 2, 3, A, B, C, D to 125th Street

Black music history was made here every night, and they're still churning out new stars at the legendary Wednesday talent nights.

THE CLOISTERS/ FORT TRYON PARK

ℹ Fort Washington Avenue at Margaret Corbin Plaza, Washington Heights

✆ 212-923-3700

☼ March–Oct 9.30am–5.15pm Tues–Sun; Nov–Feb 9.30am–4.45pm Tues–Sun

www.metmuseum.org

Ⓜ Subway A to 190th Street

A beautiful version of a medieval monastery, this offshoot of the Met is set in the wilderness that is Fort Tryon Park. It contains a huge amount of booty from Middle Ages Europe, including sculpture, religious paintings and stained glass.

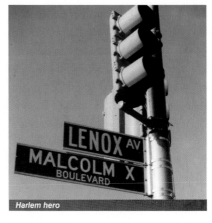
Harlem hero

INWOOD HILL PARK

ℹ 207th Street with Seaman Avenue

✆ 212-304-2365

Ⓜ Subway A to 190th Street, 1, 9 to 207th Street

This wild overgrown park at the very uppermost tip of Manhattan is where to come when you're not in that New York state of mind, as it provides the perfect escape from the madness of Downtown.

MORRIS-JUMEL MANSION

ℹ 65 Jumel Terrace between 160th and 162nd Streets

☼ Wed–Sun 10am–4pm

Ⓜ Subway A, C to 163rd Street

Ⓥ $3

See what New York was like before it got its independence, at this pre-revolutionary mansion.

TOM'S RESTAURANT

ℹ 2880 Broadway at 112th Street

✆ 212-864-6137

☼ Daily 6–1.30am

Ⓜ Subway 1, 9 to 110th Street-Cathedral Parkway

Ⓥ Two courses $10

Worth a look only if you're in the area anyway, mainly because it's where *Seinfeld* et al used to chew the fat.

What goes around, comes around at Coney Island

Brooklyn and Queens

If you're in New York for a week, then the island of Manhattan
should keep you so busy that you won't want to go off and
discover the outer boroughs of Brooklyn, Queens, the Bronx
and Staten Island. In each of NYC's outer four boroughs you'll
find attractive architecture and some interesting places to eat if
you know where to look. Why not restrict yourself to Brooklyn,
the best of the outer boroughs, and Queens, now that the
Museum of Modern Art has temporarily relocated there?

A DAY OUT IN BROOKLYN

If you do feel like getting off the island, then take the Brooklyn Bridge
wooden walkway – an experience in itself – and head for the Brooklyn
Heights Promenade for a breathtaking view of the Manhattan skyline.
Brooklyn Heights is a good place for a wander just to get a flavour of the
area and you're bound to find somewhere nice for coffee on Montague
Street. If you want to get to the heart of Brooklyn, take subway B-Q to
Prospect Park where you'll be able to have a row on the lake, a look at the
Brooklyn Botanic Garden and visit the Brooklyn Museum of Art, an 'out
there' museum that faced down Mayor Giuliani, who tried to cut off its
funding when it displayed a controversial exhibition of New British
Artists.

Two places you must check out, even if you're not up for the whole
boroughs experience, are Brighton Beach, a run-down Russian enclave
on the ocean, and Coney Island – both weird and wonderful places to
visit. After checking out the Beach's locals in all their sequinned and fur-
coated glory, stroll along the infamous boardwalk down to Coney Island.
Coney Island is grim and you should only go if you're prepared to laugh
at the rusted-up fairground rides, disgusting-looking seaside hot dogs
and the sheer grunge that greets you on your way back to the subway
station. Fun can be had, especially on the rollercoaster, a rickety and
extremely scary affair, and in the 'freak' shows, where a slightly short lady
sitting in a box qualifies as an attraction.

A DAY OUT IN QUEENS

The journey from 42nd Street Station on the 7 local train to the new
MoMA building in Queens is one of the great journeys you can take in
New York. Not only do you get a fantastic view of the Midtown
skyscape as you emerge from the tunnel, but the sight of the dereliction
of Queens is a real cinematic moment.

Get off at 33rd Street station – you'll already see the rooftop museum

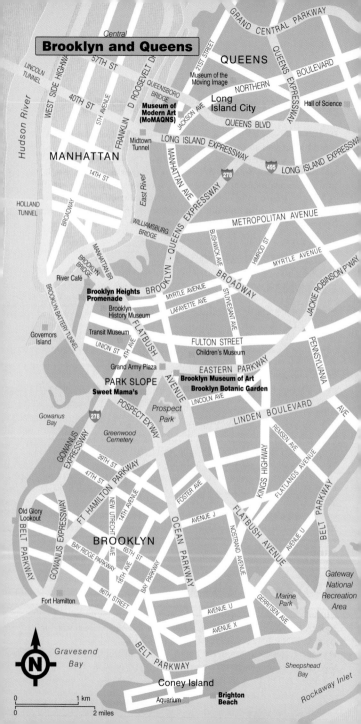

signs from your elevated subway train – and you've got MoMA QNS, as it's being called (*see p. 15*). Sweet Mama's is a dyke-owned eatery on Park Slope, a suburb of Brooklyn that boasts a massive gay and lesbian population. Serving traditional, belly-filling Southern food like fried chicken and catfish in kitsch surroundings. Flatters The Famous dinner for two is $40. No credit cards accepted.

The familiar gothic arches of Brooklyn Bridge

OUTLINES

BROOKLYN HEIGHTS PROMENADE

From Cranberry Street to Remsen Street, entrance at Montague Street

BROOKLYN MUSEUM OF ART

200 Eastern Parkway

718-638-5000

www.brooklynart.org

Wed–Fri 10am–5pm; Sat–Sun 11am–6pm

Subway 2, 3 to Eastern Parkway-Brooklyn Museum

Free

A surprisingly edgy art museum. Everything from ancient Egypt to Rodin.

MOMA QNS

45–20 33rd Street at

Queens Boulevard (from spring 2002–late 2004)

www.moma.org

Subway 2, 3 to Eastern Parkway-Brooklyn Museum, Subway 7 to 33rd Street; N to Queensboro Plaza, transfer to 7 train to 33rd Street

The world's greatest modern art museum.

The biggest in the world

All Shopped Out

If you can't buy it in New York, then it's probably not for sale. It may have some cool skyscrapers and be the world centre for culture of all types, but shopping is what New York is really for, as far as most visitors are concerned. You even get to choose your own shopping vibe. You can cruise the arty boutiques of SoHo and spend a small fortune on designer loveliness, lose all sense of propriety up on Fifth Avenue – though breakfast at Tiffany's is not an option, unless you take your own, that is – or check out the bargains (and the tat) down in the Village. You'll find a level of service unheard of in Europe and plenty of great record and bookstore 'finds' to counteract the blandness of the megastores.

Top of the Shops

Abercrombie and Fitch

🛈 A&F at South Street Sea Port,199 Water Street. *See map p. 28*
📞 212-809-9000 www.abercrombie.com 🚇 Subway J, M, Z, 2, 3, 4, 5 to Fulton Street

Annoyingly located at the south of Manhattan in the Seaport area (get a cab if you can), A&F is definitely worth the trek. More upmarket than Gap, and only available in the States, the cute college-style T-shirts and sweat pants scream 'I've been holidaying in NYC'.

Banana Republic and Old Navy

🛈 Banana Republic: 552 Broadway, between Spring and Prince Streets. *See map p. 28*
📞 212-925-0308 www.bananarepublic.com 🕐 Mon–Sat 10am–8pm; Sun 11am–7pm
🚇 Subway N, R to Prince Street; L to 6th Avenue
🛈 Old Navy: 610 6th Avenue at 18th Street. *6th Ave and 18th: map p. 40*
📞 212-645-0663 www.oldnavy.com 🚇 Subway F to 14th Street

ALL SHOPPED OUT

Banana Republic is always a cause of great excitement to visitors from Europe mainly because we haven't got one (it's in the pipeline for London). From the makers of Gap, it's a slightly upmarket version, with basics and accessories of great quality. At the other end of the Gap family is Old Navy, the cheeky, cheap and cheerful younger brother. You may sneer as you walk into the usually over-crowded, self-consciously eccentric stores, but there are usually anything up to ten items, some as cheap as $10, that you've somehow just got to have.

Barnes & Noble

ℹ 1972 Broadway at the Lincoln Center. *See map p. 56*
✆ 212-595-6859 www.bn.com
☻ 9am–midnight **Ⓜ** Subway 1, 2, 3, 9 to 66th Street-Lincoln Center

This is New York's main chain of bookstores, and there are branches pretty much all over town. Especially good is the one up on Broadway above Columbus Circle. It has five floors of tomes with a café at the top handily next to the news-stand so you can leaf through their magazines while you top up on caffeine. It's all a bit woody and fake, but there's no beating the sheer volume of goods on display.

Barney's New York

ℹ 660 Madison Avenue, at 61st Street. *Map p. 50* **✆** 212-826-8900
www.barneys.com **☻** Mon–Fri 10am–8pm; Sat 10am–7pm; Sun 11am–6pm
Ⓜ Subway N, R to 5th Avenue or 4, 5, 6 to 59th Street

You can trawl round the big-name designer stores downtown or you can come to Barney's and find eight floors of designer menswear all in one location. It's
names, names, names,
with everyone from
Armani to Yamamoto
represented as well as
a whole floor
devoted to more
conservative ties and
smart-but-casuals.
Obviously, the prices
are prohibitive, but if
you're intent on
designer loveliness
and only have so
much time to devote
to it, this is where
that credit card

Designer menswear

takes a bashing. And when you've shopped till you just can't shop no more, there's Fred's, a funky little restaurant in the basement to perk you back up (see *p. 93*).

Dave's

🛈 581 Avenue of the Americas (6th Avenue) between 16th and 17th Streets. *6th Ave and 16th: map p. 40* **📞** 212-226-6800

🚇 Subway 1, 2, 3, 9, F to 14th Street; L to 6th Avenue

You can try out Canal Jeans on Broadway, but if you're here for cheap Levi's and Carhartt's and Schott jackets, there's no better place than Dave's. Fully relocated and refurbished, it's a yawning chasm of bargains, with jeans going for as little as $20. Straightforward and unglamorous – well, here this stuff is just workwear, not fashion – Dave's always has all the sizes and the friendly beardy staff will almost literally fall over themselves to make sure you get everything you want. With recent changes in the tax laws meaning there's nothing added to clothes prices under $100, there's no way you're coming out of Dave's without a couple of huge brown paper bags full of bargains. A New York institution.

Sign of a bargain

Dean & DeLuca

🛈 550 Broadway at Prince Street. *Map p. 28*
📞 212-431-1691
🕑 Mon–Sat 10am–8pm; Sun 10am–7pm
🚇 Subway N, R to Prince Street

A brilliant chain of coffee shops which spin off into delis, the flagship is undoubtedly the SoHo store on the corner of Broadway and Spring. Containing everything from little boxes of edible petals and fruits you've never heard of, let alone seen, to huge hunks of Belgian chocolate, rare teas that look like flower heads, freshly made fruit tarts and... well, you get the picture: Dean & DeLuca is a foodie's idea of nirvana. Great for presents (their own-brand New York Coffee for instance), and there's even a little espresso bar at the front where you can cool your heels.

ALL SHOPPED OUT

Kiehl's

ⓘ 109 3rd Avenue between 13th and 14th Streets. *3rd Avenue and 13th: see map p. 34* **ⓐ** 212-677-3171
☯ Mon–Sat 10am–6.30pm (until 7.30pm Thu, 6pm Sat)
Ⓜ Subway: L to 3rd Avenue; N, R, 4, 5, 6 to 14th Street-Union Square
All credit cards accepted

Since 1851 Kiehl's has been one of the weirdest and most wonderful shops you'll find in New York. The top-class moisturisers and conditioners may be sold in places like Liberty's in London and Barney's here, but this is where the world's supermodels call in to stock up. The no-fuss plastic bottles line the walls of this double-storefront emporium, but so do weird signed photographs of people climbing Everest to try out conditioners at high altitudes and horses enjoying the Kiehl's equine range. Totally unselfconsciously bonkers, the staff are the most helpful anywhere and will bung you a big handful of samples if you buy anything. A little pricey but a total must.

Pop Shop

ⓘ 292 Lafayette Street between Houston and Prince Streets. *See map p. 28.*
ⓐ 212-219-2784 www.haring.com **☯** Tues–Sat noon–7pm; Sun noon–6pm
Ⓜ Subway B, D, F, Q to Broadway-Lafayette Street; 6 to Bleecker Street

Moss

ⓘ 146–150 Greene Street between Houston and Prince Streets. *See map p. 28*
ⓐ 212-226-2190
www.mossonline.com; email: store@mossonline.com
☯ Tues–Fri 11am–7pm; Sat noon–7pm; Sun noon–6pm
Ⓜ Subway B, D, F, Q to West Houston Street

In a town with some great interiors stores (you must check out Totem), Moss is a little SoHo jewel of a shop with some real finds. Whether you're in the market for some glassware of unparalleled beauty, an Arne Jacobson clock to go with your chairs, or even a weird soap dispenser that looks like the blood bags they use on *ER*, this is your

American graffiti

It's looking a bit 80s but still remarkably contemporary, and for gay history, art and some great little presents to bring back you can't do a lot better than graffiti artist Keith Haring's Pop Shop. A tiny little store over on Lafayette, it's done out – floor, ceiling and walls – in Haring's trademark glowing babies and barking dogs (makes a great photo) and sells any amount of knick-knacks with similar designs going on all over them. It'll only take you ten minutes to do it, and if it's good enough for Madonna...

CLOTHING

ABERCROMBIE AND FITCH

See p. 67.

APC

ℹ️ 131 Mercer Street between Prince and Spring Streets

☎️ 212-966-9685

🕐 Mon–Sat 11am–7pm; Sun noon–6pm

Ⓜ️ Subway N, R to Prince Street

Ultra-swish in a pared-down way, this SoHo store is the epitome of downtown cool. Great basic-with-a-twist clothing will set you back an arm and a leg with a little room at the back filled with pricey novelty items.

CANAL JEANS

ℹ️ 504 Broadway between Spring and Broome Streets

☎️ 212-226-1130

www.canaljean.com

🕐 Daily 9.30am to 9pm

Ⓜ️ Subway: N, R to Prince Street; 4, 5, 6 to Spring Street; B, D, F, Q to Broadway-Lafayette

Legendary multi-storey jeans emporium with great bargains in denim and undies for men, women and kids, and an extensive vintage and army surplus section downstairs. It's a bit of a bun-fight, especially at sale time; but you'll be hard pressed to beat it.

CENTURY 21

ℹ️ 22 Cortlandt Street between Broadway and Church Street

☎️ 212-227-9092

🕐 Mon–Fri 7.45am–8pm; Sat 10am–7.30pm; Sun 11am–7pm

Ⓜ️ Subway N, R, 1, 9 to Cortlandt Street; 2, 3, J, M, Z, 4, 5 to Fulton Street

Bargain jeans

ALL SHOPPED OUT

Huge, stress-inducing store buried in designer clothes. There's much more rubbish than treasure, and the jury's still out on some of the 'designers', but if you're in a jumble-sale mood, it's fine.

DAVE'S
See p. 69.

H&M
ℹ️ 1328 Broadway at 34th Street and Herald Square
🚇 212-564-9922
www.hm.com
🕐 Mon–Sat 10am–9pm; Sun 10am–8pm
🚇 Subway B, D, F, Q, N, R to 34th Street-Herald Square

Eyebrow-raisingly cheap fashion that won't last you the season, even if it does look like real Miu Miu. There were queues round the block when the first NYC branch opened.

STUSSY
ℹ️ 140 Wooster Street between Houston and Prince Streets
🚇 212-995-8787
www.stussy.com
🚇 Subway N, R to Prince Street

This new concrete-floored temple of street-sound loveliness for wannabe homeboys is much

airier than the old store on Prince, and while it's upped the glamour stakes – Eames footstools in the changing rooms! – the staff defy you to unfold their $26 T-shirts. Ridiculously-priced luggage on the upper floor.

DESIGNER CLOTHING

CALVIN KLEIN
ℹ️ 654 Madison Avenue at East 60th Street
🚇 212-292-9000
🕐 Mon–Sat 10am–6pm (to 8pm Thu); Sun noon–6pm
🚇 Subway 4, 5, 6 to 59th St, N, R to Lexington Avenue

Mr Klein's superstore and is as delicious as the clothing within.

DKNY
ℹ️ 655 Madison Avenue at 60th Street
🚇 212-223-3569
www.dkny.com
🕐 Mon–Sat, 10am–7pm (9pm Thu); Sun noon–6pm
🚇 Subway 4, 5, 6 to 59th Street, N, R to Lexington Avenue

Great store, with some great clobber, as well some quirky little touches like the staff's favourite records and a magazine bar. You can even grab a fresh juice while you're shopping.

DOLCE & GABBANA
ℹ️ 825 Madison Avenue between 68th and 69th Streets
🚇 212-249-4100
www.dolcegabbana.it
🕐 Mon–Sat 10am–6pm (7pm Thu)
🚇 Subway 6 to 68th Street-Hunter College

Of course our favourite homo designers, friends of Madonna *et al*, have a presence in NYC.

EMPORIO ARMANI
ℹ️ 110 5th Avenue at 16th Street
🚇 212-727-3240
www.emporioarmani.com
🕐 Mon–Sat 11am–8pm (7pm Sat); Sun noon–6pm
🚇 Subway L, N, R, 4, 5, 6 to 14th Street-Union Square

Beautifully tailored Italian classics.

GUCCI
ℹ️ 685 5th Avenue at 54th Street 🚇 212-826-2600
🕐 Mon–Sat 9.30am–6pm (7.30pm Thu); Sun noon–6pm
🚇 Subway E, F to 5th Ave

Gucci's Manhattan branch is pretty much like any other. Generally only watches will work out cheaper than in Europe.

PRADA
ℹ️ 841 Madison Avenue at 70th Street

📷 212-327-4200

www.prada.com

⏰ Mon–Sat 10am–6pm (7pm Thu)

Ⓜ Subway 6 to 68th Street-Hunter College

Gorgeous Italian fashions and surly staff.

PRADA SPORT

ⓘ 116 Wooster Street between Prince and Spring Streets 📷 212-925-2221

www.pradasport.com

⏰ Mon–Sat 11am–7pm; Sun noon–6pm

Ⓜ Subway N, R to Prince Street; C, E to Spring Street

Shop for sporty-style Italian apparel, and then nip downstairs to eat in the groovy Canteen (see *p. 80*).

VERSACE

ⓘ 647 5th Avenue between 51st and 52nd Street 📷 212-317-0224

www.versace.com

⏰ Mon–Sat 10am–6pm (–7pm Thu)

Ⓜ Subway 6 to 51st Street

Opulent, brash and brassy – and that's just the staff.

CLOTHING CHAINS

The following are flagship stores. Check the phone book for branches.

ARMANI EXCHANGE

ⓘ 645 5th Avenue at 51st Street

📷 212-980-3037

www.armaniexchange.com

Ⓜ Subway E, F to 53rd Street

Armani's diffusion range of casual wear, unavailable in the UK, is young and fresh. It's a little over-branded but worth checking out.

BANANA REPUBLIC

See p. 67.

Designer Donna Karan is one of New York's giants

Stylish shop front

department stores, but still well worth a wander, especially for the Barbie Boutique on the fifth floor and the 'oh so New York' Little Brown Bag you get with purchases. And the restaurant in the basement is a good, lowish-priced stop-off.

MACY'S
ℹ 151 West 34th Street between 7th Avenue and Broadway
☎ 212-695-4400
www.macys.com
🕙 Mon–Sat, 10am–8.30pm; Sun 11am–7pm
Ⓜ Subway B, D, F, N, Q, R to 34th Street-Herald Square

It may be huge, but that doesn't necessarily mean good. OK, so there's miles of menswear – everything from very street to so smart your dad would wear it – but it's often over-crowded, always seems to be going through some renovation or other, and the staff lack the service skills of other department stores.

SAKS FIFTH AVENUE
ℹ 611 5th Avenue between 49th and 50th Streets
☎ 212-753-4000
🕙 Mon–Sat 10am–7pm

CLUB MONACO
ℹ 160 5th Avenue at 55th Street
☎ 212-352-0936
www.clubmonaco.com
Ⓜ Subway E, F to 5th Avenue

Cleaning up on the preppy casuals front, with safe clothes at safe prices. The slacks, coats and straight-down-the-line shirts pick up on fashion trends. Check out the fabulous accessories.

OLD NAVY
See p. 67.

URBAN OUTFITTERS
ℹ 628 Broadway between Bleecker and Houston Streets
☎ 212-475-0009
www.urbn.com
🕙 Mon–Thu 11am–9pm; Fri–Sat 11am–10pm; Sun 11am–8pm

Ⓜ Subway 6 to Bleecker Street; B, D, F, Q to Broadway-Lafayette

This is worth checking out, not just for cheap here-today fashions but for wacky one-offs like their recent jewel-encrusted heavy metal T-shirts.

DEPARTMENT STORES

BARNEYS
See p. 68.

BLOOMINGDALE'S
ℹ 1000 3rd Avenue at 59th Street
☎ 212-705-2000
www.bloomingdales.com
🕙 Mon–Sat 10am–8.30pm (7pm Sat); Sun 11am–7pm
Ⓜ Subway N, R to Lexington Avenue; 4, 5, 6 to 59th Street

Not the greatest of the

(Thu 8pm, Sat 6pm);
Sun noon–6pm
Subway B, D, F, Q to
47th–50th Streets-
Rockefeller Center; E, F to
53rd Street

The ground floor is
deliciously woody in
an old-skool way –
and you get greeted at
the door by a nice
lady! But don't let that
fool you that they're
out of touch. Go up to
men's contemporary,
and you'll see they're
completely up to the
minute, if not the
second.

MUSIC AND BOOKS

BARNES & NOBLE

See p. 68.

BLEECKER STREET RECORDS

239 Bleecker Street at
6th Avenue
212-255-7899
Mon–Thu 11am–
10pm; Fri–Sat 11am–1am;
Sun 11am–10pm
Subway 1, 9 at
Houston Street; B, D,
F, Q, A, C, E to West
4th Street

Collectors will get
moist in this Village
store that has so
many undreamt-of
delights (though it
really doesn't look
like anything special
when you walk in).

Get bootlegs of
concerts you missed,
remixes you couldn't
afford all put onto to
one handy CD, and
demos you didn't
even know existed.

COLONY

1619 Broadway at
49th Street
212-265-2050
www.colonymusic.com
Mon–Sat 9.30am–
1am; Sun 10am–midnight
Subway N, R to 49th
Street; 1, 9 to 50th Street

If you're short on
Barbra Streisand wine
or Madonna coat-
hangers, Colony is
your shop. A frankly
bizarre and messy mix
of Broadway and
karaoke CDs –
including opera! – and
some rare collector
schmutter and sheet
music, Colony is
where the Beatles and
Elvis shopped.

DIA CENTER FOR THE ARTS BOOKSTORE

548 West 22nd Street
between 10th and 11th
Avenues
212-989-5566
www.diacenter.org
Wed–Sun noon–6pm
during Sept–June season
Subway C, E to 23rd
Street

A great selection of
arts books – one of
the greatest in the city,
with CDs and maga-
zines that you can dip
into while lounging
around on the couches
in this dazzling tiled
store attached to a
very funky art space.
Just don't try to take a
photo of those crazy
tiles: they'll have your
hand off.

FOOTLIGHT

113 East 12th Street
between 3rd and 4th
Avenues

Saks appeal

ALL SHOPPED OUT

📞 212-533-1572
www.footlight.com
🕐 Mon–Fri 11am–7pm;
Sat 10am–6pm; Sun closed
Ⓜ Subway L, N, R, 4, 5, 6
to 14th Street-Union Square

Anything in the way of soundtracks or cast recordings or big old diva vocalists can be found in this well-stocked showbizateria, which also has some rare recordings that will make your heart race, a load of sale items, and a good stock of Judy Garland fanzines.

FORBIDDEN PLANET

ℹ️ 840 Broadway at 12th Street 📞 212-473-1576
🕐 Mon–Sat 10am–10pm; Sun 11am–8pm
Ⓜ Subway L, N, R, 4, 5, 6 to 14th Street-Union Square

If it's a statuette of Buffy the Vampire Slayer you're after, or maybe a collector's item horror comic, check out this sci-fi outlet peopled by nerds of all ages, creeds and colours. An absolute must if you are into all things spacey, horrific and collectible.

METROPOLITAN OPERA SHOP

ℹ️ Lincoln Center, 136 West 65th Street at Columbus Avenue

📞 212-580-4090
🕐 Mon–Sat 10am–2nd interval (around 8–9pm); Sun noon–6pm
Ⓜ Subway 1, 9 to 66th Street-Lincoln Center

Opera lovers will swoon at this emporium stacked with signed diva photos, hard-to-come-by CDs and DVDs, and any amount of operatic knick-knacks. If you have opera-queen mates, it's a one-stop gift shop.

SATELLITE

ℹ️ 342 Bowery between Bond and Great Jones Streets
📞 212-780-9305
www.satelliterecords.com
🕐 Mon–Sat 1–9pm; Sun 1–8pm
Ⓜ Subway 6 to Bleeker Street; B, D, Q to Broadway-Lafayette; N, R to Prince Street-Broadway

If you've come to NYC for dance vinyl, boogie on over to this airy temple of beats complete with its 20 listening stations and very-clued-up staff who, if you give them a clue about what you're into, will start playing you products. Taking in all dance styles, Satellite even has a specialist area for CDs (don't you love that!).

TOWER RECORDS

ℹ️ 1961 Broadway at 66th Street
📞 212-799-2500
🕐 Daily 9am–midnight
Ⓜ Subway 1, 9 to 66th Street-Lincoln Center

Record buying in New York can be disappointing (you're expecting so much!), but this three-storey Upper West Side superstore has some great stock, good specialist areas, a café and a good DVD section.

GROOMING

CREED

ℹ️ 9 Bond Street between Broadway and Lafayette Street
📞 212-228-1940
🕐 Mon–Tues 11.30am–7.30pm; Wed–Sat, 11.30am–8pm; Sun noon–6pm
Ⓜ Subway 6 to Bleeker Street

Totally gorgeous perfumery that comes from England via Paris with an amazing interior and displays that make it seem like a Scent Museum. Check the comedy celebrity chairs, ask for your free sample and discuss the customised fragrance service.

KIEHL'S

See p. 70.

SEPHORA

ⓘ 555 Broadway between Prince and Spring Streets

☎ 212-625-1309

⏱ Mon–Sat 10am–8pm (Thu–Fri 9pm); Sun noon–7pm

Ⓜ Subway 6 to Spring Street

Perfume junkies will swoon at this cosmetic superstore, which has scents and make-up lined up in strictly alphabetical order, great décor and chairs for partners who can't be bothered to spend hours spraying scent onto bits of card. You'll come out headachy and stinking.

INTERIORS

THE TERENCE CONRAN SHOP

ⓘ Bridgemarket, 407 East 59th Street between First and York Avenues

☎ 212-755-9079 www.conran.com

⏱ Mon–Fri 10am–8pm; Sat 10am–7pm; Sun noon–7pm

Ⓜ Subway N, R to Lexington Avenue; 4, 5, 6 to 59th Street

Mr Conran's two-floor modernist palace of loveliness is brimming over with the right chairs, tables and kitchenware plus some great present ideas that fit in a

Totem

suitcase. Also worth checking out are the shopping/dining deals with Conran's brilliant Guastavino's restaurant next door.

TOTEM

ⓘ 71 Franklin Street between Broadway and Church Street

☎ 212-925-5506 www.totemdesign.com

⏱ Mon–Sat 11am–7pm; Sun noon–5pm

Ⓜ Subway 1, 9 to Franklin Street

Another gorgeous interior design store, with items imported from the world over. There are some sexy, transportable items.

GAY STUFF

GIRL PROPS

ⓘ 153 Prince Street at West Broadway

☎ 212-505-7615

www.girlprops.com; email: sohot@erols.com

⏱ Mon–Fri 9am–11pm; Sat–Sun 10am–11pm

Ⓜ Subway N, R to Prince Street.

If you're after a cut-price sequined bikini, a feather boa or some glittery hair accessories, this is your spot. A tiny store that's great for bargain gifts.

THE NOOSE

ⓘ 261 West 19th Street, at 8th Avenue

☎ 212-807-1789

⏱ Tue–Wed 11am–8pm; Thur–Fri 1–8pm; Sat 11am–8pm; Sun 1–7pm

Ⓜ Subway: 1, 9 to 18th Street

It's tiny but this Chelsea fetish store has the waterfront covered when it comes to collars, chains and piercings.

Brasserie – talk of the town

Eating Out

New York is the world centre for great nosh, whether it's an organic doughnut from Dean & DeLuca with your coffee or a full-scale glamour blow-out at one of the city's hip restaurants. Food from around the globe is represented, portions tend to be large and the service immaculate. And remember, it never hurts to make a reservation.

Cream of the Cuisine

A Salt and Battery

ℹ️ 112 Greenwich Avenue at Horatio Street. *Greenwich Ave and Horatio Street: see map p. 34* 📞 212-691-2713 🕐 Noon–10pm daily

🚇 Subway A, C, E to 14th Street; L to 8th Avenue 🍴 🍴

If you're missing the old country you can't get any better comfort food than some nice fish and chips wrapped in newspaper served by someone with a bit of chirpy Cockney patter going on. This brilliant tiled takeaway does the finest cod and big fat soggy English chips in town as well as haddock and sole, while you can even treat yourself to a chip butty smothered in proper malt vinegar – in addition to any of the wittily named sandwich dishes on the menu.

Brasserie

ℹ️ 100 East 53rd Street between Park and Lexington Avenues. *East 53rd St: map p. 44* 📞 212-751-4840 🕐 Lunch 11.30am–3.00pm; dinner 5.30pm–1.00am; Sun until 10.00pm

🚇 Subway E, F to Lexington Avenue; 6 to 51st Street 🍴 🍴

The following price guides have been used for eating out and indicate the price for a main course:

🍴 = cheap = under $10

🍴 = moderate = $10–$20

🍴 = expensive = over $20

The talk of New York is how they turned the already high-tone Brasserie into the best-looking restaurant in the city. Come down the glass gangplank into the centre of a jaw-droppingly glamorous room of bent-wood beauty with walls of frosted glass, 15 webcam screens showing punters coming in, and booths separated by diagonal pistachio leather-padded walls. Jostly even early in the week, Brasserie runs the gamut from big piles of red meat to seven-vegetable cous cous, with desserts mainly a glamorous twist on favourites like apple pie and mousse. And it may be sheer coincidence, but they always seem to seat you in an area with other gay men and lesbians, which is nice.

Canteen

 142 Mercer Street at Prince Street. *Mercer St/Prince St: see map p. 28*

212-431-7676
www.CANTEENnyc.com

Tues–Sat 12.00pm–2.00am; Sun–Mon 12.00pm–12.00am

Subway N, R to Prince Street; 6 to Spring Street

Bursting with glamour

Perfectly placed in the centre of SoHo, right under the new Prada store on the corner of Mercer and Prince Streets, Canteen is bursting with New York glamour and the kind of staff that just can't be nice enough.

Filled with funky orange art works (apparently, they're chairs) and circular free-standing booths, the Canteen vault dining area does lunch, dinner, brunch and late candlelit suppers until 2 in the morning. Although it is slightly pricey it's not ridiculous, and you can have anything from down-to-earth pizza to sophisticated fennel bisque with parmesan croutons. The seafood specials, which include oysters on the half-shell, are especially recommended.

Diabla

202 9th Avenue at 22nd Street. *9th Avenue/22nd Street: see map p. 40*
646-638-1111 Subway C, E to 23rd Street

From the makers of Food Bar and probably the most fun you can have in a restaurant on a Saturday evening, Diabla is a lively and very stylish Mexican serving all the regular burrito/fajita Tex-Mex favourites. The front bar is lively, the restaurant (very Ralph Lauren Homeware meets mad Mexican style) is even livelier, with pretty much everyone gay and in party mood.

It will never win any prizes for the food, but for niceness and fun and sheer *joie de vivre*, you can't touch it. Plans are afoot to turn it into a party venue, so make sure you phone to check on the current situation before you set off for dinner here.

Brunch at the Food Bar

Food Bar

🛈 149 8th Avenue between 17th and 18th Streets. See map p. 40
📞 212-243-2020; fax 212-691-0695
🍴 Breakfast all day;
lunch Mon–Fri 11am–4pm;
dinner 5pm–11.30pm
🚇 Subway A, C, E to 14th Street; L to 8th Avenue; 1, 9 to 18th Street
🍴 💲 – 💲

Ideally situated just on the main Chelsea drag on Eighth Avenue, Food Bar is the place for a brunch if you've had a hard and heavy one the night before. With huge windows that swing right open in the summer, the place is large and airy and super-kitschly done out (check out the Virgin Marys on the way to the bathroom). They do dinner and lunch, and the place is packed on a lovely summer evening. But the brunch is the thing, with a fixed price that includes something eggy, coffee, juice, muffins and even a Bloody Mary if you're not quite ready to throw in the towel.

Florent

🛈 69 Gansevoort Street between Greenwich and Washington Streets. *Gansevoort Street/Washington Street: see map p. 34.*
📞 212-989-5779
🕐 Mon–Thu 9am–5am; Fri–Sun open 24 hours
🚇 Subway A, C, E, to 14th Street; L to 8th Avenue
🍴 💲 – 💲

Open 24 hours a day at the weekend, Florent has been serving up diner fare with a twist to a very funky crowd of Chelsea boys and arty girls for decades. Go through the plastic butcher's curtain and you'll find a long bar, some of the worst lighting in town and one of the best atmospheres. At Formica tables you'll find customers who have had to fight to get in gobbling down burgers and fries and fancier French food. It's one venue in the district that looks like it had something to do with the meat-packing industry.

The atmospheric Florent

Guastavino's

ℹ 409 East 59th Street at First
Avenue. *East 59th Street/First Avenue:
see map p. 50* **☎** 212-980-2455
www.guastavinos.com
🕐 Mon–Sun 11.30am–2.30pm,
5.30pm–11pm **🚇** Subway N, R to
Lexington Avenue; 4, 5, 6 to 59th Street
🍴 💳

Named America's best new
restaurant by *Esquire* magazine, Sir

Terence Conran has certainly
made a splash with this Parisian-
style brasserie restaurant under the
Queensboro Bridge with its
soaring ceilings and capacity of
300 people. If you'd prefer
something a little more intimate,
choose a table in the club upstairs,
which boasts better food than the
busy, must-book brasserie. Expect
everything that you would from a
typical Conran venture – formal
French dishes in a busy *fashionista*
favourite.

Once Upon A Tart

ℹ 135 Sullivan Street between Prince and Houston Streets. *See map p. 28* **☎** 212-
387-8869 **🕐** Mon–Fri 8am–8pm; Sat 9am–8pm; Sun 9am–6pm
🚇 Subway C, E to Spring Street **🍴 💳–💳**

If you want something quick, tasty and even quite wholesome while out
spending in SoHo, this is your place. A double-fronted affair, the left-hand
shop sells take-out, while the right-hand one has ten small tables where you
can tuck into a brilliant veggie tart, sandwich, soup or salad on paper plates
and a fresh juice. In its rather beautiful original condition – bare bricks and
ancient display windows – and with staff who couldn't be cooler or
friendlier, it's also great for just a rock cake and a coffee.

Le Pain Quotidien

ℹ 100 Grand Street at Mercer Street. *See map p. 28* **☎** 212-625-9009
www.painquotidien.com
🕐 Daily 8am–7pm
🚇 Subway J, M, N, R, Z, 6 to Canal Street
Also at: 1336 1st Avenue at 72nd Street; 833
Lexington Avenue at 64th Street; 1131
Madison Avenue at 84th Street; 50 West
72nd Street at Columbus Avenue
🍴 💳–💳
🚫 credit cards not accepted

Two-roomed eatery with a vast
back room with refectory-style
seating. Old-school breakfast snacks
including boiled egg and soldiers

Daily bread

and their delicious home-made chocolate spread; plus the coffee comes in a bowl. During the day you can get a great sandwich.

Pastis

ⓘ 9 9th Avenue at Little West 12th Street. *9th Avenue/Little West 12th Street: map p. 34*
📞 212-929-4844 email frontdesk@pastisny.com 🕐 Breakfast Mon–Fri 9am–10am;
lunch Mon–Fri noon–6pm; dinner Mon–Fri 6pm–midnight; brunch Sat–Sun 10am–5pm;
dinner Sat–Sun 5pm–midnight Ⓜ Subway A, C, E, to14th Street; L to 8th Avenue

The pseudo-French bistro décor might be a bit rustic for some tastes (if you can see it through the crowds that is), but make no mistake, Pastis is the place to be, if you can get in. There are two huge rooms and a terrace (weather permitting) where you'll find crowds of smart New Yorkers and in-the-know tourists tucking into basic French fare at prices that really aren't bad considering it's owned by the same guy that brought you the super-expensive Balthazar's. Don't be surprised if you are asked to wait at the bar. Just do it; it's worth the wait. Especially recommended is the weekend brunch.

A taste of France in New York

Best of the Rest

LOWER MANHATTAN, CHINATOWN, LITTLE ITALY AND LOWER EAST SIDE

DONUT PLANT

🛈 379 Grand Street between Essex and Norfolk Streets

📠 212-505-3700

⏰ Tues–Sun 6.30am–6.30pm

Ⓜ Subway B, D, Q to Grand Street; F to Delancey Street

🍴 🍽

Not a restaurant, not even a café, the Donut Plant is the front to a doughnut factory, and there really isn't much more than a single seat and a plant. The friendly Hispanic ladies dish up the most delicious and nutritious flavoured doughnuts, but it's a long way to go, so sample their wares at a handier Dean & DeLuca.

71 CLINTON FRESH FOOD

🛈 71 Clinton Street between Stanton and Rivington Streets

📠 212-614-6960

⏰ Mon–Thu, 6pm–10.30pm; Fri–Sat 6–11.30pm

Ⓜ Subway F to Delancey Street; J, M, Z to Essex Street

🍴 🍽

Another fabulous eatery on the Lower East Side, 71 Clinton is great to take a gang out to. Divinely hip, this place attracts a young, cool, boisterous Manhattan crowd. You'll definitely need to book, and you'll need to book before 5pm as they don't take reservations after that. There are a couple of walk-in tables available, but expect to queue along with the rest of the city's hipsters. Delicious American menu with some great veggie options.

SOHO AND TRIBECA

BOULEY BAKERY

🛈 120 West Broadway at Duane Street

📠 212-964-2525

⏰ 11.30am–3pm, 5.30pm–11.30pm

Ⓜ Subway A, C, 1, 2, 3, 9 to Chambers Street

🍴 🍽

With only 20-odd covers, you'll need to book in advance for this miniature version of celebrity chef David Bouley's original restaurant. The food's fabulous, and makes up for the almost rough-and-ready décor. The fusion-like menu beckons with dishes such as salmon with a sesame seed crust. Check out the much cheaper grub in the adjoining bakery, where you can enjoy fantastic pizza and delicious sandwiches for a fraction of the price.

CANTEEN
See page 80.

CHURCH LOUNGE
ⓘ Tribeca Grand Hotel, 2 Avenue of the Americas at White Street
☏ 212-519-6500
⌚ Daily 12pm–3am
Ⓜ Subway 1, 9 at Franklin Street

The beautiful Tribeca Grand Hotel seats diners in the vast Atrium Lounge. The menu has a slight Mediterranean feel, the service is wonderful, and the waiting staff are handsomely dressed in black. We couldn't keep our eyes off them or the oh-so-sexy décor.

FANELLI'S
ⓘ 94 Prince Street at Mercer Street
☏ 212-431-5744
Ⓜ Subway N, R to Prince Street; 6 to Spring Street

Either a dive or a bit of a real New York find, depending on your outlook. Fanelli's is a very old-school bar/restaurant with sport constantly on the TV and food in the form of straightforward burgers and pasta with a few fancier French items. There are waxed checked tablecloths and an ornate dark-wood bar.

JUNIPER
ⓘ 185 Duane Street between Greenwich and Hudson Streets
☏ 212-965-1201
⌚ 11am–4pm, 5.30pm–10pm
Ⓜ Subway 1, 9 to Franklin Street

One of the most romantic little restaurants in Manhattan, Juniper is

dark and beautifully lit with real French staff who get quite a little atmosphere going in here, especially on Saturday nights. The lunch menu is crammed with croques and pastas, while at night there is a range of modern brasserie fare.

MERCER KITCHEN
ⓘ Mercer Hotel, 99 Prince Street at Mercer Street
☏ 212-966-5454
⌚ Daily 8–10.45am, 12–2.45pm, 6pm–midnight
Ⓜ Subway N, R to Prince Street; 6 to Spring Street.

Beyond hip, attracting sexy young Manhatannites. The menu – from seafood platters to basic pizzas changes daily.

Good enough to eat

EATING OUT

ODEON

 145 West Broadway between Duane and Thomas Streets

212-233-0507

Sun–Thu 11.45am–2am; Fri–Sat 11.45am–3am; Sun 11.30am–2am

Subway A, C, 1, 2, 3, 9 to Chambers Street

A veritable New York institution and probably the best restaurant downtown, Odeon is known for its traditional Frenchified décor and grill-style menu. Pop in for a spot of light lunch – specialities are your basic burgers and tuna steaks. A good one if you want it to feel a bit special, but try to book.

LE PAIN QUOTIDIEN

See page 82.

THE SCREENING ROOM

 54 Varick Street at Laight Street

212-334-2100

Mon–Thu 12–3pm; daily 5.30pm–11pm; Fri–Sat 5.30pm–midnight; Sun 11.30am–3.30pm

Subway 1, 9 to Canal Street

A cute little concept: enjoy film-themed cocktails in the bar and sumptuous dishes in the restaurant – check out the $30 *prix fixe* menu – or settle down to an arthouse movie or classic flick in the 1940s-style movie theatre. Look out for gay favourites like the highly popular re-runs of classics like *Breakfast at Tiffany's* during brunch.

GREENWICH VILLAGE

BENNY'S BURRITOS

113 Greenwich Avenue at Jane Street

212-727-3560

A Salt and Battery – a great place for fish and chips

Daily 11.30am–
midnight
 Subway A, C, E, L,
1, 2, 3, 9 to 14th Street-8th
Avenue

Cheap, in every sense
of the word, this kitsch
Mexican eatery is
crowded out with
Jackie O lamps,
Mexicana and
Village hipsters
chowing down on
delicious burritos and
drinking out of plastic
cups.

FLORENT
See page 81.

LUPA
🛈 170 Thompson
Street between
Bleecker and Houston
Streets
🌀 212-982-5089
🕒 Daily 5–11.30pm
💻 Subway 1, 9 to
Houston Street
🍴 🏠

With its traditional
Italian décor and
whirring ceiling fans,
Lupa is about as
straightforward (in a
good way) as it gets if
you're after a basic
Italian in romantic
surroundings.

NL
🛈 169 Sullivan
Street between Houston
and Bleecker Streets
🌀 212-387-8801
💻 Subway A, C, E, B, D,

F, Q to West 4th Street-
Washington Square
🍴 🏠

This dinky, beautifully
done out little place is
Manhattan's only
Dutch restaurant and
has a bit of a canteen
feel. The food is a
strange mix of
sauerkraut risottos and
monkfish carpaccio,
while the guys who
run it are young and
full of fun.

PASTIS
See page 83.

RHONE
🛈 63 Gansevoort Street
between Greenwich and
Washington Streets
🌀 212-367-8440
🕒 Daily 6pm–midnight
💻 Subway A,C,E to 14th
Street, L to 8th Avenue
🍴 🏠

Rhone has everything
you would expect
from the area: bare-
brick and plaster,
candles, jazz, designer
furniture, great-looking
staff and a great range
of food – from bites to
blow-outs – that you
can eat at the central
bar or at one of the
usually-all-booked-up
tables up front. It's on
the pricey side, but
expect an eclectic
menu with risottos,
rabbit, fondue,
sweetbreads. There's
also a bar/lounge.

RISOTTERIA
🛈 270 Bleecker Street
between 6th and 7th
Avenues
🌀 212-924-6664
💻 Subway A, C, E, B, D,
F, Q to West 4th Street-
Washington Square; 1, 9 to
Christopher Street-Sheridan
Square
🍴 🏠

An absolute find, this
tiny, wood and
brushed-steel restaurant
runs like a canteen,
where you order from
the counter then take
your seat, and offers
millions of varieties of
gorgeous risotto and
salads piled up
skyscraper-high. A real
lunch must.

CHELSEA

THE BIG CUP
🛈 228 8th Avenue
between 21st and
22nd Streets
🌀 212-206-0059
💻 Subway C, E to
23rd Street
🕒 Mon–Fri 7am–1am;
Sat-Sun 8am–2am
🍴 🏠

Famous and popular
with the gay Chelsea
crowd, The Big Cup
is fine if it's just a
quick inter-purchase
coffee you're after.
The place is done out
in day–glo, which
produces a self-
consciously boho
atmosphere. There's

EATING OUT

coffee and tea and smoothies and brownies and muffins, and a crowd of Chelsea boys that range from young and skatey to old and arty.

BLUE WATER GRILL

 31 Union Square West at 16th Street

212-675-9500

Subway L, N, R, 4, 5, 6 to 14th Street-Union Square

Mon–Sat 11.30am–4pm 5pm–12.20am (1am Fri–Sat); Sun 10.30am–4pm, 5pm–midnight

Most punters prefer the cavernous upstairs eating area here, but don't overlook the lower level with its jazz club-like atmosphere. A good raw bar, delicious lobster and a great selection of fresh fish make this a very special night out. Blow the budget and book in advance.

CHELSEA GRILL

135 8th Avenue between 16th and 17th Streets

212-242-5336

Wed–Sat 11.30am–4am; Sun–Tues 11.30am–2am

Subway A, C, E to 14th Street

Smack bang in the heart of Chelsea, the

Grill is a traditional dining room that serves up great burgers. A bit on the dingy side, it attracts a mixed gay-straight crowd and is great for people-watching if you can bag a window seat. Open nice and late in the week, it also appeals to the post-bar crowd and has a garden for those hot summer nights.

COLA'S

148 8th Avenue between 17th and 18th Streets

212-633-8020

Subway A, C, E, L to West 14th Street

As near a trad Italian restaurant as you'll find on the main drag of gay Chelsea, Cola's is tiny, intimate and friendly. The menu has all your pastas and mains such as grilled salmon and Tuscan veal stew. The clientele of all ages is almost exclusively gay.

DIABLA
See page 80.

EAST OF EIGHTH

254 West 23rd Street between 7th and 8th Avenues

212-352-0075

Mon–Thu

11.30am–10.00pm; Fri–Sat 11.30am–5.00pm; Sun 5.00pm–10.00pm

Subway 1, 9, C, E to 23rd Street

Famous and somewhat overrated, the big news about this basic American restaurant is that is has a patio. The staff are lovely, but the food is your basic pasta/pizza/half-hearted Mexican and the décor dreary. Mind you, it manages to scare up quite a nice – and very gay – atmosphere.

EMPIRE DINER

210 10th Avenue at 22nd Street

212-243-2736

24 hours, except Tues closed 4am–8.30am

Subway C, E to 23rd Street

A must-see classic American diner in its original state with gum-chewing waitresses (and gay waiters). Big with club kids trying to soak up some of the alcohol.

FOOD BAR
See page 81.

MESA GRILL

102 5th Avenue between 15th and 16th Streets

A classic American diner

📞 212-807-7400

🌐 www.mesagrill.com

🍽 Lunch Mon–Fri
noon–2.30pm;
brunch: Sat–Sun
11.30am–3pm;
dinner Mon–Sun
5.30pm–10.30pm

Ⓜ Subway L, N, R, 4, 5, 6
14th Street-Union Square

🍴 💳

💳 credit cards accepted

This brightly coloured
South-Western
restaurant with its
comedy cowboy
furniture and high-
impact décor is noisy
and lively. It also has a
famous chef producing
up-to-scratch fare for
the up-for-it crowd.

LA PETITE ABEILLE

ℹ️ 107 West 18th Street at
the corner of 6th Avenue

📞 212-604-9350

🌞 Mon–Fri 7am–7pm;
Sat–Sun 9am–6pm

Ⓜ Subway F, L to West
14th Street

Also at: 400 West 14th
Street; 466 Hudson;
134 West Broadway

🍴 🍴–💳

This cute little
Belgian eatery with
bright décor and
Tintin posters serves
up a great Sunday
brunch, as well as
some gourmet-
standard snacks,
soups, home-made
quiches and sarnies.

Busy at lunchtime
with workers more
than tourists, it's a
canteen affair and
you can sit up at the
window and watch
the world go by.

REPUBLIC

ℹ️ 37 Union Square West
between 16th and 17th
Streets

📞 212-627-7168

🌞 Thu–Sun noon–
midnight; Sun–Wed
noon–11pm

Ⓜ Subway L, N, R,
4, 5, 6 to 14th Street-Union
Square

🍴 💳

Canteen-style filling
and service, reasonably

Go Dutch at NL

MIDTOWN

AMY'S BREAD
 672 9th Avenue between 46th and 47th Streets

212-977-2670

Mon–Sat 11.45am–2.15pm, 6–10.30pm (no lunch Sat); Mon–Fri 7.30am–11pm; Sat 8am–11pm; Sun 9am–4:00pm

Subway C, E to 50th Street. Also at 75 Ninth Avenue between 15th and 16th Streets

priced noodles and soups in a brash, noisy setting. Enjoy some fabulous Japanese ramen and listen to other people's conversation. Too many kids at the weekend, but quite a few gay waiters.

TOCQUEVILLE
15 East 15th Street between 5th Avenue and Union Square West

212-647-1515

Mon–Sat 11.45am–2.15pm 6–10.30pm (no lunch Sat)

Subway L, N, R, 4, 5, 6 to Union Square

Cosy yet plush little pistachio and orange restaurant serving up high-end grub at high-end prices. This is a quiet, quality little eatery, with white tablecloths,big

bouquets on the bar, and unusual treats like creamless purée of butternut squash soup with seared duck foie.

WILD LILY TEA ROOM
511A West 22nd Street at West Side Highway

212-691-2258

Tues–Sun 11am–10pm

Subway C, E to 23rd Street

Way out west towards the piers, the arty, zeny Wild Lily Tea Room is a lovely little find. A Japanese bare-brick-and-orchid eatery with a little goldfish pool at the front, it serves 41 varieties of tea alongside such delights as carrot purée soup, grilled fish and exotic vegetable curry.

Get a taste of old Manhattan for breakfast (even though it only dates to 1992) at this old-style bakery with more choice than most of us can cope with before coffee. Scones, muffins, applesauce doughnuts, sourcream coffee cake with a selection of baguettes and sandwiches for lunch. There are only a few tables to perch at, but it's worth a try.

ASIA DE CUBA
237 Madison Avenue between 37th and 38th Streets

212-726-7755

Mon–Wed 12pm–11.30pm; Thu–Fri 12pm–12am; Sat 5.30pm–12am; Sun 5.30pm–11pm.

Subway 4, 5, 6, 7 to 42nd Street-Grand Central

In Ian Schrager's delicious hotel Morgans (see *p. 128*), this is a total New York, *Sex and the City*-style experience with gorgeous design by Phillipe Starck. An interesting Latin/Asian fusion menu attracts Manhattan's hottest restaurant-goers, so it can be a little on the intimidating side.

BRASSERIE

See page 79.

CHEZ JOSEPHINE

 414 West 42nd Street between Ninth and Tenth Avenues

212-594-1925

Subway A, C, E to 42nd Street

A gay Manhattan institution and an old fave of Jackie O, this theatreland restaurant is pure showbiz. Dark and grand and a little tatty around the edges, it has a basic but sound menu – Chinese ravioli with goat's cheese, grilled salmon, crab cakes – and attracts an older, more flamboyant crowd, including the odd drag queen.

LE CIRQUE 2000

 Palace Hotel, 455 Madison Avenue between 50th and 51st Streets

212-303-7788

Mon–Sat 11.45am–11pm; Sun 5.30pm–10pm

Subway 6 to 51st Street; B, D, F, Q to 47–50th Street-Rockefeller Center

High-end, high-society, opulent and surreal – and that's just your fellow diners. Le Cirque 2000's mad interior sits perfectly with the truffle- and *foie gras*-heavy menu. Treat yourself to a little eccentric Manhattan dining and join the multi-aged hipsters.

EATERY

 798 9th Avenue at 53rd Street

212-765-7080

Lunch Mon–Fri noon–4pm; brunch Sat–Sun 11am–4pm; dinner Mon–Thu 5pm–midnight; Fri–Sat 5pm–1am; Sun 5pm–11.30pm

Subway C, E to 50th Street

One of the funky new eating places that's emerging in the revamped Hell's Kitchen, Eatery is spacious, modern and popular with the local gay residents for its e-bar (big on Thursdays). The décor is straight from *Wallpaper,* and the

food is a huge, adventurous selection ranging from tofu vegetable salad to plum ginger tartlette.

GRAND CENTRAL STATION OYSTER BAR

 Lower Level, Grand Central Terminal 42nd Street at Park Avenue

212-490-6650

Mon–Fri 11.30am–9.30pm; Sat 5.30pm–9.30pm

Subway 4, 5, 6, 7 to 42nd Street-Grand Central

Corny but romantic, with amazingly fresh seafood and a price tag to match. A huge vaulted space decorated with opulent dark wood. You'll feel like you're on a film set, and a glass of the bubbly stuff is a must.

HELL'S KITCHEN

 679 9th Avenue between 46th and 47th Streets

212-977-1588

Lunch Mon–Fri 11.30am–3.30pm; dinner Sun–Wed 5pm–11pm; Thu–Sat 5pm–midnight

Subway C, E to 50th Street

For Mexican that's not all burritos and re-fried beans, Hell's Kitchen is a gourmet affair.

EATING OUT

Chic and dark with a great bar to wait for a table at (and you'll probably have to). Hell's Kitchen is designer-y with its wine-bottle chandeliers, but still has a nice local feel to it.

HUDSON CAFETERIA

 356 West 58th Street between 8th and 9th Avenues
212-554-6000
Breakfast 6.30am–11am daily; lunch and dinner 11.30am–1am daily
Subway A, B, C, D, 1,

9 to 59th Street-Columbus Circle

Eating doesn't come much swisher than this. With long refectory tables and model-like waiters, it's a feast for the eye. The food is pricey and ranges from macaroni cheese to snapper. Do it on the cheap for breakfast.

ORSO

322 West 46th Street between 8th and 9th Avenues
212-489-7212
Mon, Tues, Thu, Fri,

noon–11.45pm; Wed, Sat, Sun, 11.30am–11.45pm
Subway A, C, E to 42nd Street-Port Authority

This famous media restaurant is bordering on poky, but still attracts an older theatre-biz crowd, mainly for the buzzy atmosphere. The food is basic Italian and the prices rather high.

UPPER WEST SIDE

EPICES DU TRAITEUR

103 West 70th Street

The swish Hudson Cafeteria

between Columbus Avenue
and Broadway

 212-579-5904

Mon–Thu
5.30–10.30pm;
Fri–Sat 5.30pm–midnight

Subway 1, 2, 3, 9 to
72nd Street

If you've had enough
of American brasserie
fare, this North
African/Mediterranean
gem will be a breath
of fresh air. Staff can be
slack, but it's worth it.

UPPER EAST
SIDE

FRED'S

 Barney's, 660
Madison Avenue at 61st
Street

212-833-2220

Mon–Thu
5.30–10.30pm;
Fri–Sat 5.30pm–midnight;
Mon–Thu 11.30am–8.30pm;
Fri–Sun 11.30am–5.30pm

Subway N, R to 5th
Avenue or 4, 5, 6 to 59th
Street

At lunchtime it's one
of the most fun
places to be. Busy and
buzzy with food from
crab cakes to latkes.

NICOLE'S

Nicole Farhi,
10 East 60th Street
between 5th and
Madison Avenues

212-223-2288

RESTAURANT
FINDER

American
Amy's Bread	90
The Big Cup	87
Canteen	80
Chelsea Grill	88
The Donut Plant	84
East of Eighth	88
Eatery	91
Empire Diner	88
Florent	81
Food Bar	81
Fred's	93
Hudson Cafeteria	92
Mesa Grill	88
Odeon	86
Le Pain Quotidien	82
The Screening Room	86
71 Clinton Fresh Food	84
Tocqueville	90

Asian
Asia de Cuba	90
Republic	89
Wild Lily Tea Room	90

Belgian
La Petite Abeille	89

Dutch
NL	87

French/
Brasserie
Bouley Bakery	84
Brasserie	79
Chez Josephine	91
Guastavinos	82
Le Cirque 2000	91
Florent	81
Juniper	85
Mercer Kitchen	85
Nicole's	93
Pastis	83
Rhone	87

Fusion
Church Lounge	85
Epices du Traiteur	92

Italian
Cola's	88
Lupa	87
Orso	92
Risotteria	87

Seafood
Blue Water Grill	88
Canteen	80
Grand Central Station Oyster Bar	91

South
American
Benny's Burritos	86
Diabla	80
Hell's Kitchen	91

Mon–Sat 10am–10pm;
Sun noon–4pm

Subway N, R to
5th Avenue

As swish as the store
it's in, this award–
winning restaurant
combines glamour
with good food.

At your service

Out on the Town

New York nightlife is going through a bit of a crisis at the moment, mainly due to the campaigning of former-Mayor Giuliani, whose 'clean up the town' mission meant cleaning up most of the gay nightlife. With his hard line on drugs, a lot of the huge dance clubs have found it impossible to survive, while strict new rules on raunchy behaviour have meant that what was once the wildest nightlife in the world has been brought (excuse the pun) to its knees. Some of the racier clubs soldier on and have to forego the selling of alcohol, while others have just given up the ghost. On the bright side, the lounge and bar scenes have never been better, with gorgeous new watering holes opening all the time. And don't go out without your passport: you never know when they're going to want to see proof of age for drinking dens, even if you are in your late 30s. Remember that things change fast in NYC, so always pick up a copy of *HX* or *Next* to keep up to the minute on developments and special parties.

My Top Clubs and Bars

Barrage

ⓘ 410 West 47th Street between 9th and 10th Avenues. *West 47th Street: map p. 44*
☎ 212-586-9390 Ⓜ Subway C, E to 50th Street

Okay, so it's just a bar. But it's a very nice one and it's blazing a trail up in Hell's Kitchen. Spacious and modern, with hundreds of sexy pictures of male models made into an art installation round the walls, Barrage is very friendly: turn to anyone and talk and they'll talk right back. Friday or Saturday it's queued up outside, but probably worth the wait.

OUT ON THE TOWN

G

ℹ️ 225 West 19th Street between 7th and 8th Avenues. *W 19th Street/7th Avenue: map p. 40*

📞 212-929-1085

🕐 4pm–4am; cash only

🚇 Subway 1, 9 to 18th Street

For a while G was the main destination for any guy in Chelsea with muscles and a vest to show them off. Now, with the arrival of Heaven and XL, it's lost a bit of its headstart but is still usually packed out with party boys (and men). The huge oval bar at the rear has barmen who are scrupulously fair about who's next in line, while the DJ keeps things hopping.

Heaven

ℹ️ 579 6th Avenue between 16th and 17th Streets. *Map p. 40*

📞 212-243-6100

🚇 Subway F to 14th Street; L to 6th Avenue

This new addition to the lounge scene at the location of the much-loved King is not quite as swish as it thinks it is. Done out all in white with three floors of fun to be had, Heaven (no relation to the London superclub) plays host to a variety of nights all detailed in *HX* and the like. The crowd are notable for their friendliness, though the whole thing might be a bit dolly for some tastes.

G – the place for party boys

Heaven!

La Nueva Escuelita

ℹ 301 West 39th Street at 8th Avenue.
West 39th Street/8th Avenue: map p. 44
☎ 212-631-0588 www.escuelita.com
☀ Thu–Sun
Ⓜ Subway A, C, E to 42nd Street-Port Authority Bus Terminal **$** Entry $5

This could just be your best night out in New York. A mad and crazy Hispanic drag club big on salsa, merengué and Latin house, and featuring performances by the totally wigged-out divas of Escuelita, its Thumpin' Thursdays and Spicy Fridays are regulars in the gossip columns for their sheer exuberance, go-go boys and pulling power. The last Thursday of the month they play host to the Black Inches party. And you can imagine what that means.

Pop Rocks!

ℹ Thursdays at 219 Flamingo, 219 2nd Avenue at 13th Street. *2nd Avenue: map p. 34*
☎ 212-462-9077 www.poprocksnyc.com
☀ From 10pm **Ⓜ** Subway L to 3rd Avenue, 6 to Astor Place
$ Entry $3

New York has been relatively slow to pick up on the whole young thing, but Pop Rocks! more than makes up for it. The DJ is 21 years old, the revellers dancing to Britney and Christina and Madonna often younger still, and the atmosphere something like the school disco you always dreamed about. Also, if you're over 21 and can prove it, there are lots of drinks promotions so you could get drunk for free.

Pork

ℹ️ Wednesdays At The Lure, 409 West 13th Street between Greenwich and Washington Streets. *West 13th Street/Greenwich Street: map p. 34*

🌀 212-741-3919

🕐 10pm–4am

Ⓜ️ Subway A, C, E to 14th Street; L to 8th Avenue

Here is a great venue that is huge and very rough-and-ready with a shop! The crowd of up-for-it guys are all done out in their finest fetishwear (and rough old T-shirts and jeans and boots and... you get the picture). Unfortunately, due to the restrictions the whole thing is a bit on the tame side. But the punters try their hardest and definitely give you a night off from the buff Chelsea crew.

Roxy on Saturdays

ℹ️ 515 West 18th Street between 10th and 11th Avenues. *West 18th Street: map p. 40* 🌀 212-645-5156 www.roxynyc.com

🕐 Sat from 11pm

Ⓜ️ Subway A, C, E to 14th Street; L to 8th Avenue

Roxy pretty much has the dance scene to itself at the moment. Just as well it's okay in a shirts-off-arms-in-the-air kind of way. Victor Calderone (of Madonna remix fame) rules the main floor, while there is pop and disco and new wave in the Martini Lounge. Considering New York used to be the place of the legendary nightclub, it's far from cutting-edge, but it is still possible to have a good night out.

Cocktail hour

XL

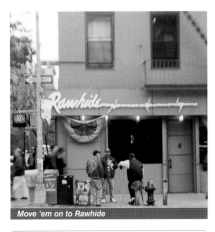

357 West 16th Street between 8th and 9th Avenues. *West 16th Street: map p. 40* 212-995-1400 www.xlnewyork.com 4pm–4am Subway A, C, E, L to 8th Avenue

Is this the most gorgeous gay bar in the whole world? It could be. With a giant fish tank in the toilets, projected clouds scudding across the curved ceiling and an avant-garde light show changing the exquisite retro chairs in white leather from pink to lavender to sky blue, XL is a feast for the eyes before the buffed-up clientele even arrive. On two floors, it really is a total must, especially at happy hour Mon–Fri, 4–9pm.

Move 'em on to Rawhide

Splash

50 West 17th Street between 5th and 6th Avenues
212-691-0073
4pm, dancing from 10pm–4am
Subway 1, 2, 3, 9 to 14th Street
Free weekdays   happy hour 2-for-1 4–9pm

It's been around the block a bit, but Chelsea's premier bar-dancing joint is still big with the locals. On two floors, with a front bar, a bigger back bar and a dancefloor, Splash still seems to fill up pretty well, even when they impose a $10 entry fee at weekends. Cruisey, but not uncomfortably so, Splash attracts men of most ages, some of them with women friends in tow. It has lots going for it – a general lively atmosphere, a popular dancefloor and beefy barmen in very skimpy shorts. But it's the guys in G-strings dancing for tips on the bar (or in the bar-top showers that gave the joint its name) that keep pulling in the punters after all these years.

For the alternative crowd

All Clubbed Out

GREENWICH VILLAGE

BAR D'O

 29 Bedford Street at Downing Street

 212-627-1580

 Subway 1, 9 to Houston Street

Scary New York drag queens Joey Arias, Raven O and Sherry Vine bring you the ultimate in cutting-edge cabaret from their cosy hangout. Try not to stick out – they'll have you – but do stick around for Joey's amazing 'channelling' of Billie Holiday.

BEIGE

 At B Bar, 40 East 4th Street at Bowery

 212-475-2220

 Subway 6 to Astor Place

Once the be-all-and-end-all must-do Tuesday nighter, Beige is still enticing a modelly fashion crowd out midweek to hear an eclectic mix of tunes. Worth going just to check out the once-famous Bowery bar, but make sure you dress right up; this is one of the few places in Manhattan that insists on it.

THE COCK

 188 Avenue A at 12th Street

 212-946-1871

 Subway L to 1st Avenue; N, R, 4, 5, 6 to 14th Street-Union Square

Don't get any ideas from the name, this mad-as-a-hatter East Village bar is many things but not that. The Cock really comes alive on a Saturday, when they give you Foxy Dollars to vote for your favourite in the talent contest. Expect the likes of Jackie Beat to preside. A mad one, but a good one.

CRAZY NANNY'S

 21 7th Avenue South at Leroy Street

 212-366-6312

www.crazynannys.com

 Subway 1, 9 to West Houston Street

One for the locals, this pub-style bar is a virtually boy-free zone (apart from drag queens, if they count) and offers drag king nights, a pool table and local perfomance acts. A bit rough, but very ready and with a late 20s/early 30s mixed-race bunch.

LOVERGIRL

 At True, 28 East 23rd Street between Madison Avenue and Park Avenue South 212-254-6117

www.lovergirlnyc.com

 Subway 6, N, R to 23rd Street

Attracting a gorgeously multi-racial crowd, the Lovergirl venue, with its sexy lighting and two floors of fun, is a rowdy, fun-filled night boasting some of NYC's sexiest go-go girls. Hot, sweaty and pumping, if you're in NYC on a Saturday night you really shouldn't miss it.

Always carry ID...

MEOW MIX

🛈 269 East Houston Street at Suffolk Street between Avenues A and B

📞 212-254 0688

🕐 Mon–Fri 5pm–4am; Sat, Sun 3pm–4am

Ⓜ Subway F to 2nd Avenue

Friendly, busy neighbourhood girl bar offering Xena nights, live bands, cheap beer and cheap décor. Tatty round the edges, it's one for the alternative crowd and don't be surprised to find members of Luscious Jackson down there.

THE MONSTER

🛈 80 Grove Street at Sheridan Square

📞 212-924-3558

🕐 Daily from 10pm; from 2pm on Sun

Ⓜ Subway 1, 9 to Christopher Street-Sheridan Square

With its piano for singalongs, this Village institution is a bit on the old-school camp side for some tastes and does tend to attract the less cutting-edge characters from the gay scene, but that said, it does have quite a funny Sunday tea dance complete with go-go dancers and is the only place round these parts with a dancefloor.

STONEWALL

🛈 53 Christopher Street between 6th and 7th Avenue South

📞 212-463-0950

Ⓜ Subway 1, 9 to Christopher Street-Sheridan Square

Yes, it's a piece of history and not a bad bar if you like it cosy and bricky and not-too-glam. There are exhibits and cuttings about the riots, a little back bar and a glitzier upstairs dancefloor where there are go-go boys sometimes.

CHELSEA

BARRACUDA

🛈 275 West 22nd Street between 7th and 8th Avenues

📞 212-645-8613

🕐 Daily 4pm–4am

Ⓜ Subway 1, 9 to 23rd Street; C, E to 23rd Street

Extremely popular in the local punters' polls, this is a long narrow bar with pool tables at the back and a bit of a 1950s vibe going on. The clientele is a mixed 30-something bag and includes those here for the long haul and those stopping off on their way to somewhere much more glamorous.

FOOD BAR
See page 81.

HEAVEN
See page 96.

HELL
 59 Gansevoort Street between Greenwich and Washington Streets
212-727-1666
Subway A, C, E to 14th Street or L to 8th Avenue

If you are getting tired of men in vests and wall-to-wall house music, Hell will be like a breath of fresh air. Large and dark with chandeliers with red bulbs, the music can be anything from the Smiths to Madonna to some Mexican chanteuse. The crowds on the banquettes are 20s/30s, slightly

alternative and often accompanied by women friends.

J'S HANGOUT
675 Hudson at 14th Street Subway A, C, E to 14th Street

A very cheeky (and fairly dingy) little club where almost anything goes. Free drinks to guys in jockstraps, money off if you have a gym card, and a free clothes check. (See the *Getting Off* section of *HX* for more specialised clubs and events.)

RAWHIDE
212 8th Avenue at 21st Street
212-242-9332
www.rawhide-nyc.com
Mon–Sat from 8am; Sun from noon
Subway C, E to 23rd Street

Small and dark – even

at midday – the only real light comes from the pinball machines around the walls. Look out for beer blasts and go-go boys that go beyond the call of duty. The crowd is mixed but on the older side at this spit and sawdust joint.

SPLASH
See page 99.

WEST SIDE SAUNA
See page 112.

XL
See page 99.

MIDTOWN

BARRAGE
See page 95.

CHASE
255 West 55th Street at 8th Avenue 212-333-3400 Subway A, C, B, D, 1, 9 to 59th Street-Columbus Circus; B, D, E to 7th Avenue

This dinky but swishy little Midtown bar is responsible for bringing some of the Chelsea crowd up to Hell's Kitchen. There are two levels of modern décor, nicely turned-out punters and cocktails, but it can be quiet on weekdays.

GAIETY
201 West 46th Street at Broadway
212-391-9806 and

Take your pick . . .

Where you can be wicked...

212-221-8868

🌀 Shows 1.30pm,
3.30pm, 6pm, 8.30pm,
10.30pm; Fri–Sat Marathon
6.15pm, 9.15pm, 12.15am

Ⓜ Subway N, R, S, 1, 2,
3, 7, 9 to Times Square

💲 $15

Not a bar or a club, but
a strip joint and the
one where Madonna
shot some of her *Sex*
book. Very beautiful
model-type guys get
down to business in the
clean and comfortable
surroundings, with free
punch and a lounge
where you can chat
with the performers
after the show. A real
eye-opener.

THE WHISKEY

ⓘ Paramount Hotel, 235
West 46th Street

Ⓜ Subway C, E to 50th
Street, or N, R, S, 1, 2, 3, 7,
9 to Times Square-42nd
Street

This bar is in the
ultra-chic Paramount
hotel designed by
Philippe Starck. Check
out the beautiful hotel
reception. Then make
your way to the bar
for a candlelit cocktail
where you can listen
to hip sounds. This was
once one of the
trendiest hangouts in
town. Although it is a
little past its prime, this
is still a good option

for a quiet pre-party
drink.

WHISKEY BLUE

ⓘ W New York, 541
Lexington Ave at 49th Street

☎ 212-755-1200

Ⓜ Subway E, F to
Lexington Avenue, or 6 to
51st Street

If the burly guys on the
door let you in, this is a
real delight (but a little
low on the gay count).
The dimly-lit room is
set up with tables and
beds where you and
whoever you are with
can lounge decadently
around on while being
served cocktails and
enormous drinks.

Bright lights, big city

Playing Around Town

Well, it's got Broadway in it, so you would think that New York must be good for theatre. It's also the home of popular music. So, be it blockbusting musicals or tiny four-men-and-a-dog off-off-off Broadway, rock concerts or jazz recitals, NYC has pretty much got it covered, although you'll probably find, with the traffic between Broadway and London's West End being so busy, a lot of the long-running productions are fairly familiar: *The Lion King*, *Les Miserables*, *Chicago*, *Mamma Mia* and any number of less crowd-pleasing West End serious theatre productions that are trying their luck on New Yorkers.

For tickets for theatre and gigs, you can contact one of the agencies like TicketMaster or Telecharge – their websites also act as good 'what's on' guides for when you're planning your trip. Alternatively, you can try for one of the two and a half million discounted tickets sold annually at TKTS up on Broadway. Here, if you're prepared to queue, you can get tickets with up to 50% off (but with a $2.50 admin fee) for same-day performances, though you can only pay with cash or travellers' cheques. And don't fall prey to the touts working the queues: the tickets they say they just bought at the front are not, warns TKTS, always kosher. Obviously, you can also get tickets at the venues themselves, though if you phone you'll probably be referred to one of the agencies.

Your choice of theatre is going to be dictated by your choice of play. Up on Broadway, which is basically the streets going off Broadway around Times Square, you're going to find your blockbuster musicals and crowd-pleasing comedies, such as twelve-times-Tony-winner *The Producers*. Off-Broadway and off-off-Broadway indicates not location but distance from Broadway in production terms.

The whole film scene is pretty much controlled by the giants, so when you're looking in the listings (*Time Out New York* or *Village Voice*) don't be surprised to see bad films showing everywhere and the one film you're interested in showing at a godforsaken multiplex on the wrong side of town.

Unlike other American cities, the choice for those of you who prefer arthouse-style flicks is pretty poor. Of course, if you are a film buff, try and coincide your stay with the city's annual lesbian and gay film festival.

Check *Time Out New York* or the *Village Voice* for details of performances, although even gay freebie *HX* has a fairly decent theatre section.

OUTLINES

The legendary Apollo

APOLLO THEATER

🛈 253 West 125th Street between Adam Clayton Powell Jr Boulevard and Frederick Douglass Boulevard (7th and 8th Avenues)

📞 212-749-5838

🚇 Subway 2, 3, A, B, C, D to 125th Street

Music history in bricks and mortar: the list of people who've played the Apollo reads like a Who's Who of black music. The legendary amateur night on a Wednesday is still pulling them in after all these years and, although the whole Harlem thing may be a bit heavy for some tastes, it is definitely a real New York experience.

BAR D'O

🛈 29 Bedford Street at Downing Street

📞 212-627-1580

🕙 Sun–Thu 7pm–3am; Fri–Sat 7pm–4am

🚇 Subway A, C, E, B, D, F, Q to West 4th Street, or 1, 9 to Houston Street

This tiny bar cabaret, where a stool flung in the middle of the room does stage duties, is a riot of bitchy repartee and eerily accurate Billie Holiday impressions courtesy of the masterful Joey Arias. Underground and relaxed with cocktails flowing, it's already something of a gay institution.

CARNEGIE HALL

🛈 154 West 57th Street at 7th Avenue 📞 212-247-7800 www.carnegiehall.org

🚇 Subway B, Q, N, R to 57th Street

If you've got any live albums by the likes of Judy Garland, you'll already know about this place. Still packing them in for a variety of musical styles, Carnegie works best when it's classical.

CBGB'S

🛈 315 Bowery at

The avenue I'm taking you to . . .

Bleecker Street
212-982-4052
www.cbgb.com
Subway B, D, Q, F to Broadway-Lafayette; F to 2nd Avenue; 6 to Bleecker Street

Unless you want to visit the true punk shrine, you might find the legendary CBGB's a little on the hard (and grungy) side. If, however, you're interested in new gay rock, there are occasional queer music showcases organised by Homo-Corps. Check the website at: www.homocorps.com.

CINEMA VILLAGE
22 East 12th Street between 5th Avenue and University Place
212-924-3364
Subway L, N, R, 4, 5, 6 to 14th Street-Union Square
Cash only

For those of you who can't stomach main-stream action thrillers, Cinema Village offers independent flicks and a few foreign numbers. You can also catch horror films at the weekend.

KNITTING FACTORY
74 Leonard Street between Broadway and

Church Street
212-219-3006
www.knittingfactory.com
Subway A, C, E, N, R to Canal Street; 1, 9 to Franklin Street

A downtown phenomenon if you're into underground music, the Knitting Factory is a varied music space that broadcasts some of the shows live over the internet. Don't expect big stars; do expect a real downtown muso experience.

LINCOLN CENTER
65th Street at Columbus Avenue

212-875-5400
www.lincolncenter.org
Subway 1, 9 to 66th
Street-Lincoln Center

Home to no fewer than 12 internationally acclaimed companies, including the Metropolitan Opera, the New York City Ballet, the New York City Opera and the New York Philharmonic, the Lincoln Center is a culture vulture's dream ticket. It is a modern complex, which really comes alive in the summer with outdoor performances. Ticket prices vary according to which hall you are visiting. The Metropolitan Opera house – a sight to behold even if you can't always see the stage very well – is a pricey affair, while the New York State Theater next door is far more affordable.

MADISON SQUARE GARDEN

7th Avenue at 32nd Street
212-465-6741
www.thegarden.com
Subway A, C, E, 1, 2, 3, 9 to 34th Street-Penn Station

It's the one all pop stars dream of selling out. A huge indoor sports arena (not unlike Wembley in London) where the real big hitters play. Yes, it's huge and impersonal and the act will be like an ant in the distance, but it is worth it just because it's 'The Garden'.

THE NEW FESTIVAL – NEW YORK LESBIAN AND GAY FILM FESTIVAL

212-254-7228
www.newfestival.org
email: newfest@idt.net

This massive international gay film festival takes place in the run-up to the city's Pride celebrations, and showcases some of the best gay films, with some previewed exclusively here prior to release. Check out each year's line-up and buy tickets online at their website.

NEW YORK SHAKESPEARE FESTIVAL

212-539-8750
www.publictheater.org
Subway 6 to 77th Street or B, C to 81st Street

One of the great summer treats in New York is the opportunity to see Shakespeare performed for free out in the open in Central Park. The season runs from June to August, and you are allowed two tickets per person (and if it gets rained off, you'll have to start all over again). Free tickets are distributed at the Delacorte Theater in Central Park (near Turtle

Madison Square Garden

Pond, just south of the Great Lawn). Enter by Fifth Avenue at 79th Street entrance or Central Park West at 81st Street.

RADIO CITY MUSIC HALL

6th Avenue at 50th Street | 212-247-4777; Box Office: 212-307-7171 www.radiocity.com
Subway B, D, F, Q to 47th-50th Street-Rockefeller Center

As soon as you see the legendary red neon of Radio City you'll get excited. Famous for its Christmas extravaganzas with the high-kicking Rockettes, this beautiful Art Deco hall plays host to music of all shapes and sizes. Even Oasis played here.

ROSELAND

239 West 52nd Street between Broadway and 8th Avenue
212-247-0200
Subway B, D, E to 7th Avenue; C, 1, 9 to 50th Street

The much-loved Roseland, which seems like an old-school theatre inside, recently got lots of publicity for hosting the famous Madonna preview concert. Huge and old and atmospheric, it's now coming back into its own.

On Broadway

SONY LINCOLN SQUARE & IMAX

1992 Broadway at 68th Street
212-50-LOEWS, extension 638
Subway 1, 9 to 66th Street-Lincoln Center

Massive movie 'plex' with gift shops, more popcorn than you could ever need, as well as an eight-storey IMAX screen. If that's not your thing, then there are also 12 other regular-sized affairs.

TWO BOOTS PIONEER THEATER

155 East 3rd Street at 3rd Avenue
212-254-3300
Subway F to 2nd Avenue
Cash only

This alternative arthouse cinema in the East Village is run by the Two Boots pizza company.

Bargain seats

Tickets

TKTS

Times Square BranchBroadway at 47th Street
212-221-0013
Mon–Sat for evening tickets 3–8pm; Wed, Sat for matinée tickets 10am–2pm; Sun for matinée and evening tickets 11am–closing time
Subway N, R, S, 2, 3, 9, 7 to 42nd Street-Times Square

Shooting a few baskets

Working Out

In one of the most beefed-up cities in the world, you'd better believe there are enough gyms and sporting options for you to choose between, and you don't even need to be nervous. Muscles are a way of life here, and even if you're a beginner, they'll understand your thirst for pecs.

Here is my pick of the places to run, jump and pick up things that don't need picking up.

OUTLINES

CRUNCH GYM

54 E 13th Street between University Place and Broadway

212-475-2018; class hotline 212-802-5307 www.crunch.com

Mon–Fri 6am–10pm; Sat–Sun 8am–8pm

Subway L, N, R, 4, 5, 6 to 14th Street-Union Square

$23 per day

Crunch is a huge chain, with sportswear, workout CDs, books, the works. It also has a very supportive atmosphere and a whole range of activities from Pump and Grind through SpeedRope to Sculpt. The ethos is young and hip and vibrant and, although it's not a gay gym, no one turns a hair in this or the West Village branch down on Christopher Street.

FRONT RUNNERS NEW YORK

212-724-9700 www.frontrunnersnewyork. org

Subway 1, 2, 3, 9 to 72nd Street for Rutgers Church or B, C to 72nd Street for Park entrance.

A famous and notoriously fun gay running group that coolly covers six miles (you can do less if you want) in Central Park every Saturday morning at 10am. Meet inside the park, near the Daniel Webster statue at the West Drive and 72nd Street Transverse, having dumped your bags at Rutgers Church at 73rd Street and Broadway, basement level, where you will meet back after the run (and then to lunch). There are also runs on Wednesday evenings – meet at Rutgers Church at 6.45pm. Also ask about cycling, triathlon and track and field.

NEW YORK SPORTS CLUBS

128 8th Avenue at 16th Street

212-627-0065 www.nysc.com

Mon–Fri 6am–12pm; Sat–Sun 8am–9pm

Subway A, C, E to 14th Street, L to 8th Ave or 1, 9 to 18th Street

$20 a day; $78 weekly pass

Formerly the Chelsea Gym, this large two-storey fitness centre has now been taken

WORKING OUT

The place to get fit

over by a chain, but the manager assures us it will continue to cherish its gay flavour. Major refurbishment is in the works to improve upon the already quite hardcore gym facilities. A new licence for sauna and steam has been granted, and there is also massage available. Although it's not an out-and-out gay gym, most of the members are Chelsea boyz from their 20s to their 50s.

WEST SIDE CLUB

ℹ️ Second floor, 27 West 20th Street between 5th and 6th Avenues

📞 212-691-2700

Ⓜ️ Subway F, N, R to 23rd Street

Temporary membership $10 (you must take your passport); changing rooms $14; lockers $11; rooms $14 – add $2 to all the prices at weekends. In the clampdown on racy activities in the city, West Side Club has managed to cling on due to its private members' club status. Expect steam rooms, showers and weights that are open 24 hours a day.

WOLLMAN MEMORIAL RINK

ℹ️ Central Park, 5th Avenue at 59th Street entrance

📞 212-396-1010

🗓️ Mon–Tues 10am–3pm; Wed–Thu 10am–9.30pm; Fri–Sat 10am–11pm; Sun 10am–9pm; Thu 7–9pm adults only

Ⓜ️ Subway B, Q to 57th Street or N, R to 5th Avenue

💲 $15 plus skate hire: $4 and $6.50 locker rental

More than just a health and fitness thing, this is a real New York experience (you've seen it in the movies a million times). It's much more spacious and scenic than the beautiful Rockefeller Center Rink; this is what winter in New York was made for.

YMCA VANDERBILT

224 E 47th St between 2nd and 3rd Aves

212-756-9600; www.ymcanyc.org

Mon 5am–midnight; Tues–Fri 24 hours; Sat 7am–7pm; Sun 7am–9pm

Subway S, 4, 5, 6, 7 to 42nd Street-Grand Central

$25 for a day pass

This Midtown Y has two pools (these swimmers are

hardcore, mind) a gym, a sauna, a running track and quite a mixed clientele. Also see the schedule for aerobics, circuit training and yoga classes. The fact that it's open round the clock during the week makes it perfect for those whose sleep patterns have been messed with by transatlantic flights.

YMCA WEST SIDE BRANCH

5 W 63rd Street between Central Park West and Broadway

212-875-4100

www.ymcanyc.org

Mon–Fri 6am–11pm; Sat–Sun 8am–8pm

Subway A, C, B , D, 1, 9 to 59th Street-Columbus Circle

$15 for a day pass

The West Side Branch of the YMCA may not be as ritzy as the Vanderbilt, but it's gayer, if that's what you're after. You'll find two pools, three gyms and a full programme of activities including a range of classes including circuit training and yoga classes that you can choose to participate in.

Young, hip and vibrant

Get out of Manhattan, across Brooklyn Bridge

Out of Town

There's enough to keep even the most voracious holiday-maker happy on the island of Manhattan, but if it all gets a bit much and even Central Park can't soothe those frazzled nerves, or you just want to top up that sun tan and revel in a bit of rare greenery, there are some great options.

Fire Island

ℹ Take the Long Island Rail Road (LIRR) from Penn Station (subway: 1, 2, 3, 9, B, D, F, Q to 34th Street-Penn Station).
Take the Montauk branch to Sayville ($6.50-$9.50) – you'll need to change at either Jamaica or Babylon.
LIRR information: 718-217-5477
From Sayville take a jeep ($5) to the ferry at 41, River Road, ($11 return).
Ferry information: 516-589-0810
An alternative to the train is to take a luxury coach to the ferry ($20 each way) with Islanders.
🎫 212-228-7100
www.islanderstravel.com

Live the legend that is Fire Island, the hot gay holiday village just a couple of hours from NYC. Famous in the 70s for its hedonism, the boys have grown up a little now, but there is still plenty of fun to be had. Just don't go before Memorial Day as the place is deserted.

Be careful where you go on Fire Island. You want either Fire Island Pines or Cherry Grove – the other end of this long, skinny island is a families-only affair and, as cars aren't allowed, there's no escape. Don't be surprised when you arrive to find, well, nothing much: just a few little raised cabins and wooden walkways and a minute array of businesses that all

Seaside sunset

seem to be off-licences, estate agents and pet shops.

Leave New York on the Long Island Rail Road and get off at Sayville. There, you'll be greeted by some ramshackle jeeps offering to take you to the ferry for $5. Do take one. Don't attempt to walk, as it's a real hike.

If you can't be bothered to take the train (and beware, you often have to change), you can get a luxury coach all the way to the ferry, though it only operates at weekends.

Overnight accommodation is hard to come by, as most Fire Islanders have holiday homes. In Cherry Grove try the Cherry Grove Beach Hotel, with its pool, bar and club, or the Ice Palace (631-597-6600). Expect the

dancing to go on till dawn. Or you could stay at the Botel in the Pines (631-597-6500). If all else fails, make sure you check the time of the last ferry home.

While you're there, check out the scene and go to one of the famous tea dances at the Yacht Club, have a champagne supper out on the deck by the harbour or eat at Rachel's restaurant out on the ocean. If you're on a budget – and this is no place to be watching the pennies – Michael's in the Grove is cheap-but-tasty. Expect burgers and the like, but at least you can grab a seat outside.

The big weekends are obviously Gay Pride, Memorial Day and Labor Day (see *Facts*), and there is a motorcycle run the second weekend in September,

Over the water

and a Miss Fire Island drag queen competition.

The Hamptons

ℹ️ Take the Long Island Rail Road (LIRR) from Penn Station (subway: 1, 2, 3, 9, B, D, F, Q to 34th Street-Penn Station). Take the Montauk line to either Southampton, East Hampton or Montauk (one way: $10.25-$15.25).

LIRR information: 718-217-5477

Alternatively, take the Hampton Jitney, which departs from the Upper East Side ($24).

🚍 212-936-0440.

The playground of the very rich and famous – think *Sex and the City* beside the seaside – is made up of a collection of small towns. This Long Island retreat from the madness of Manhattan attracts some of the city's biggest socialites, and their wannabe hanger-on crowd.

The Hamptons boasts some amazing beaches and awesome properties, but you'll need to book way in advance to get your hands on a lowly motel room.

For a spot of gay sunbathing, get yourself along to the beach in East Hampton, just off Further Lane and near Two-Mile Road. There's also a gay hotspot in Southampton, at Fowler's Lane and Cobb Road. If it's celebs in their trunks you're after, check

out Two-Mile Hollow beach, where you'll find the odd fashion designer and a mobile phone and laptop at every turn.

If you have managed to bag a room for the night, whether it be in a motel or with a well-connected friend, the biggest gay nightspot is Club Swamp and The Annex (516-537-3332) in Wainscott. Here you can grab a bite to eat and do a spot of dancing.

If you're up for sightseeing of sorts, check out some of the

Head for the beach

monstrous mansions owned by the likes of Steven Spielberg and Kim Basinger, or head over to Southampton, a former retreat for artists like Roy Lichtenstein, which now boasts the usual glut of antique stores and galleries. It's still kind of cute. There are many VIP-only style clubs here, and if your name's not on the list, you're not getting in. If you're wandering around in the day, keep your eye out for a passing celebrity – everyone who's anyone comes here.

Accommodation drawing the artistic crowd

Checking In

There is certainly no shortage of places to stay in New York, from the world's most expensive hotels to dinky little guesthouses and everything in between. You'll probably want to stay either in Midtown, Chelsea or SoHo, as that's where most of the action is and you'll only be commuting if you don't. On a personal preference, you might want to give the mega-hotels around Times Square a miss. They tend to be more than a little bit boring.

The Best Beds

Chelsea Hotel

ℹ 222 W 23rd Street. *Map p. 40*
☎ 212-243-3700 www.chelseahotel.com
Ⓜ Subway C, E, 1, 9 to 23rd Street.

🍴 **②** _ **③**

Hudson Hotel

More than an institution, the Chelsea is a legend with artistic credentials coming out of its ears. Dylan Thomas and Thomas Wolfe have both stayed here. A strange combination of real hotel and artsy community, you pick up the flavour as soon as you step off the street into the bohemian art gallery reception. The rooms have all the usual amenities, high ceilings and very thick walls, so you're assured a good night's rest. And don't be surprised to see a present-day heavyweight celebrity in the cocktail lounge.

The following price guides have been used for accommodation, per room per night :

① = cheap = under $75

② = moderate = $75 – $200

③ = expensive = $200 and over

Chelsea Pines Inn

 317 W 14th Street between 8th and 9th Aves. *W 14th Street/8th Ave: map p. 40* 212-929-1023; fax 212-620-5646 Subway A, C, E to 14th Street or L to 8th Ave

This basic hostelry with small rooms and very friendly staff is well-located (though W 14th is a bit of a main road) and, more importantly, clean. There are only 23 rooms, all either double or triple, and not all with private bathrooms. But if you do have to wait for a shower, at least you've got television, radio and air conditioning in your room. Be aware that prices go up during Pride week.

Colonial House Inn

318 W 22nd Street between 8th and 9th Aves. *W 22nd Street/8th Ave: map p. 40* 212-243-9669; fax 212-633-1612 www.colonialhouseinn.com; email houseinn@aol.com Subway C, E to 23rd Street breakfast included

Brilliantly located in a Chelsea brownstone, this home-from-home gay hotel has a real community feel and almost exclusively gay male residents. With art everywhere, a clothing-optional rooftop sundeck and internet access, all it's really lacking is private bathrooms (though you can get one for a supplement). With rates the same for single or double occupancy, this place is very reasonable and could be the ideal Chelsea hangout.

Chic yet shabby

Ian Schrager's stunning Hudson Hotel

Hotel 17

ℹ️ 225 East 17th Street between 2nd and 3rd Avenues. *E 17th Street/2nd Ave: map p. 40*

📞 212-475-2845; fax 212-677-8178
www.hotel17.citysearch.com

Ⓜ️ Subway: N, R, 4, 5, 6 to 14th Street-Union Square; L to Third Avenue

🛏️ ① 🛎️ cash and travellers cheques only

Shabby and badly styled hotel that somehow still manages to attract a very cool crowd – Madonna posed here for her *Sex* book, the Dandy Warhols and David Bowie have filmed videos here, and David LaChapelle has done endless fashion shoots. This place is what is known in the trade as 'shabby chic'.

Hudson Hotel

ℹ️ 356 W 58th Street between 8th and 9th Avenues. *Map p. 56*

📞 212-554-6000; fax 212-554-6001

Ⓜ️ Subway A, C, E, B, D, 1, 9 to 59th St-Columbus Circle

🛏️ ②

Breathtakingly beautiful, the Hudson is Studio 54 boss Ian Schrager's newest Manhattan boutique hotel, and the idea is that it brings the price down a little. There are in theory singles for under $100, but they're rather hard to come by and the rooms, it must be said, are so tiny you may just feel like you've booked into a rabbit hutch. A very gorgeously appointed rabbit hutch, mind.

CHECKING IN

Paramount Hotel

🛈 235 W 46th Street between 8th Ave and Broadway.
W 46th Street/8th Ave: map p. 44
📞 212-764-5500; fax 212-354-5237
🚇 Subway C, E to 50th Street, or N, R, S, 1, 2, 3, 7, 9 to Times Square-42nd Street ②

This is one of Ian Schrager's boutique hotels, and even the reception is a theatrical experience, with the chaise-longue from Madonna's 'Rain' video and a very dramatic staircase. The rooms are small, but what they lack in size they make up for with proper, grown-up glamour. Paintings as headboards, dramatic lighting, video machines and condoms in the mini-bar are all there just for you. Because you're worth it.

President Hotel

🛈 234 W 48th Street between Broadway and 8th Ave. *W 48th Street: map p. 44* 📞 212-246-8800; fax 212-974-3922 www.BestNYHotels.com 🚇 Subway C, E, N, R, 1, 9 to 50th Street ②

If it's a basic beige hotel you're after, the President is brilliantly located, right between Times Square and Hell's Kitchen. It gives a bad first impression with its tacky lobby, neither does it have room service. The rooms, though, are fine, and the showers great.

Lounge at the glamorous Soho Grand

Soho Grand

🛈 310 West Broadway between Canal and Grand Streets. *Map p. 28*
📞 212-965-3000; fax 212-965-3200; www.sohogrand.com
🚇 Subway A, C, E, 1, 9 to Canal St
 ③

The height of downtown glamour, the Grand is a huge, masculine hotel with something of a Batman in Gotham vibe. This was the first hotel to open in SoHo since the 1800s. The rooms are relatively large and very New York, the bar is a happening hot-spot and the service so immaculate that they'll sort you out some goldfish for your room or even nip over to the shop opposite in the middle of the night for any items you may need. There's a great restaurant popular with non-residents, so you will want for nothing. All this plus a prime SoHo location makes this a very appealing option.

Where it's fun to stay

W Hotel

ℹ️ 541 Lexington Avenue at 49th Street. *Lexington Ave/49th Street: map p. 44*
📞 212-755-1200; fax 212-319-8344
www.whotels.com
🚇 Subway E, F to Lexington Ave or 6 to 51st Street |🚶 **3**

One of the ultimate hostelries in the city is the W Hotel. Now at four locations in Manhattan, the W on Lexington is handily located for Fifth Avenue shopping sprees. As well as offering ultra-clean, modern and minimal rooms with fake fur throws, 250-thread count linen, and Aveda design, the hotel also has one of the hippest bars in the city. You can even drag yourself to the W's spa should you feel the need to relax.

YMCA Vanderbilt

ℹ️ 224 E 47th St between 2nd and 3rd Aves. *E 47th St/2nd Ave: map p. 44*
📞 212-756-9600; fax 212-756-9922
www.ymcanyc.org
🚇 Subway S, 4, 5, 6, 7 to 42nd Street-Grand Central |🚶 **1**–**2**

You can live out your Village People fantasies at this relatively up-scale YMCA, in the middle of Midtown, opposite where Andy Warhol's infamous Factory used to be. The rooms are very small – most doubles have bunk beds – and the showers communal, but it's clean and safe and fun. Downstairs you'll find a full gym, swimming pool and steam room. The West Side one is gayer, the McBurney handier, but this is the best. Do book early.

Grand Hotel

Whether you are looking for kitsch, boho, chic or funky, New York's hotels give it to you. Prices are high and space is always at a premium, but you can always get bags of personality for your money. Follow in the footsteps of famous film stars and literary lumini, stay where the models stay, or live it up in the swanky, highly designed hotels of midtown. It's up to you.

Sleeping Around

ABINGDON BED AND BREAKFAST

🛈 13 8th Avenue between West 12th and Jane Streets

🔗 212-243-5384

🚇 Subway A, C, E, L to 14th Street

 ②

This three-room B&B in the West Village is a cute and very clean way to stay in NYC – if not a little unusual. Smack bang in the heart of Greenwich Village.

ALGONQUIN HOTEL

🛈 59 West 44th Street between 5th and 6th Avenues

🔗 212-840-6800; fax 212-944-1419

🚇 Subway: Subway B, D, F, Q to 42nd Street

 ③

The very same establishment, recently renovated, that boasted the infamous Algonquin Round Table, where the legendary Dorothy Parker held court. Traditional–style rooms.

BARBIZON HOTEL

🛈 140 East 63rd Street at Lexington Avenue

🔗 212-838-5700 fax 212-888-4271 www.thebarbizon.com email@thebarbizon.com

🚇 Subway B, Q, N, R to Lexington Avenue; 4, 5, 6 to 59th Street.

 ③

Newly renovated hotel on the Upper East Side, its former residents include Grace Kelly and Sylvia Plath. A pool and health club are free for guests, its rooms are well–designed and very generous in size. If you've got money to spend, grab a Tower Suite for fabulous

To let

views of the city, especially at night.

HOTEL CASABLANCA

ℹ 147 West 43rd Street between 6th Avenue and Broadway
📷 212-869-1212
fax 212-391-7585
www.casablancahotel.com
🚇 Subway N, R, S, 1, 2, 3, 9, 7 to 42nd Street-Times Square; B, D, F, Q to 42nd Street. **🍴** ❸

A boutique hotel in the heart of the Theatre District, with Moroccan-style décor and a lovely rooftop bar. Even more lovely is the free wine served on weeknights in the lobby. Breakfast also included.

CHELSEA SAVOY HOTEL

ℹ 204 West 23rd Street at 7th Avenue
📷 212-929-9353
fax 212-741-6309
www.chelseasavoynyc.com
🚇 Subway 1, 9 to 23rd Street **🍴** ❷

The hotel sits in the heart of Chelsea and is very reasonably priced. Clean, comfortable and a little dull. But who cares when you're staying in Chelsea?

CHELSEA STAR HOTEL

ℹ 300 West 30th Street at Eighth Avenue
📷 212-244-7827
fax 212-279-9018
www.starhotelny.com
🚇 Subway A, C, E to 34th St - Penn Station.
🍴 ❶ – ❷

A hostel-cum-theme-hotel, the Chelsea Star Hotel was Madonna's first NY home, and you can even sleep in her old room for $140 a night. Very kitsch, it boasts a roof-deck and bargain dorm rooms. Room themes include Star Trek, Dali, Orbit and even Ab Fab.

DYLAN HOTEL
 52 East 41st Street between Madison and Park Avenues
212-338-0500
fax 212-338-0569
www.dylanhotel.com
Subway S, 4, 5, 6, 7 to 42nd Street-Grand Central.

This midtown boutique hotel in the Beaux Arts style opened in 2000 and boasts rooms with high, expansive ceilings, luscious décor, a beautiful restaurant and great in-room facilities.

GERSHWIN HOTEL
7 East 27th Street off 5th Avenue
212-545-8000
fax 212-684-5546
www.gershwinhotel.com
Subway N, R to 28th Street

Affordable hotel with all the basics. Attracts a Euro, arty crowd and even boasts a 'models' floor' with special rates for all those beautiful young things trying to hit the bigtime in the Big Apple.

GRAMERCY PARK HOTEL
2 Lexington Avenue at 21st Street
212-475-4320
fax 212-505-0535
www.gramercyparkhotel.com

Subway 6 to 23rd Street

This traditional–style hotel, though a little shabby in places, is still a popular place to stay because of its handy location – you even get your own key to the private park next door. Nice-size rooms.

HABITAT HOTEL
130 East 57th Street at Lexington Avenue
212-753-8841
fax 212-829-9605
www.habitat-ny.com
Subway N, R to Lexington Avenue; 4, 5, 6 to 59th Street

Budget hotel that used to be a 'women's residence', it offers smart, modern rooms, perfect for those of you who have taste – but also a budget.

HOLIDAY INN CROWN PLAZA
1605 Broadway at 49th Street
212-977-4000
fax 212-333-7393
www.cpmny.com
Subway N, R to 49th Street; C, E, 1,9 to 50th Street

Not the most beautiful hotel in the world, the place makes up for its lack of style with location – it's right in the heart of the

famous Theatre District. The higher up you go, the better the view. Bonuses include a pool and a huge health club, which attracts a somewhat gay crowd.

LIBRARY HOTEL
299 Madison Avenue at 41st Street
212-983-4500
fax 212-499-9099
www.libraryhotel.com
reservations@libraryhotel.com
Subway S, 4, 5, 6, 7 to East 42nd Street-Grand Central Terminal

Not that you'll have any time for reading when you're shopping in Manhattan, but just in case, the Library Hotel has over 6000 books, and each of the guestrooms is named after a certain aspect of the Dewey Decimal System. Oh dear. Still, a nice place to stay.

MERCER HOTEL
147 Mercer St at Prince Street
212-966-6060
fax 212-965-3838
Subway N, R to Prince Street

The Mercer sums up everything that SoHo is about; style, celebrity, money and quality. Probably the most superbly placed hotel in the whole of New York, if you've got the cash then this is one of the places to be seen. A real beauty, and the rooms are oh–so chic.

MORGANS

 237 Madison Avenue between 37th and 38th Street

212-686-0300

fax 212-779-8352

www.ianschragerhotels.com

Subway S, 4, 5, 6, 7 to East 42nd Street-Grand Central Terminal

Another Schrager property, but you can never have too many. As you'd expect, it's pretty cool, and that's reflected in the prices. *Vanity Fair* describes it as one of New York's 'handsomest' hotels, and who would argue with them? It also houses one of the city's most expensive restaurants, Asia de Cuba.

NEW YORK PALACE

 455 Madison Ave at 50th Street

212-888-7000

fax 212-303-6000

www.newyorkpalace.com

Subway E, F to 5th Avenue

This gorgeous and opulent hotel is home to the acclaimed restaurant Le Cirque 2000, and this is one of the best places to stay in NYC. Prepare your plastic for a battering.

OFF-SOHO SUITES HOTEL

11 Rivington Street between Bowery and Chrystie

212-979-9808

fax 212-979-9801

Subway B, D, Q to Grand Street; F to 2nd Avenue; J, M to Bowery.

Located on the Lower

Life is suite

East Side, the Off-Soho Suites' moniker is intended to be ironic. Good value, clean accommodation, with fully fitted kitchens. Handy for the funky bars and eateries on the Lower East Side, though it's probably best to get a cab home at night.

ROGER WILLIAMS HOTEL
131 Madison Avenue at 31st Street
212-448-7000
fax 212-448-7007
www.rogerwilliamshotel.com
Subway 6 to 34th Street

A swanky boutique hotel with gorgeous Asian-style décor. The rate includes breakfast and a dessert buffet in the evenings. Popular with bands hitting the stage in NYC.

ROYALTON HOTEL
44 West 44th Street between 5th and 6th Avenues
212-869-4400
fax 212-869-8965
www.ianschragerhotels.com
Subway B, D, F, Q to East 42nd Street

Another Ian Schrager hotel, it's fashionable and very gay with a bustling bar. Meant for the hip and trendy amongst you, you'll appreciate the stylish décor.

T MORITZ
50 Central Park South at 6th Avenue
212-755-5800
fax 212-319-9658
Subway: B, Q to 57th Street

The cheapest way to get a view of Central Park, as long as you can bear the shabbiness inside. It won't be this way for much longer, as Mr Schrager has acquired it.

60 THOMPSON
60 Thompson Street between Spring and Broome Streets
212-431-0400
fax 212-431-0200
www.60Thompson.com
Subway C, E to Spring Street

A new SoHo hotel which boasts such highlights as floor-to-ceiling leather walls, an outdoor garden café, and a gorgeous loft apartment. Well worth at least a night's stay.

TIME HOTEL
224 West 49th Street between Broadway and Eighth Avenue
212-320-2900
fax 212-245-2305
www.thetimeny.com
Subway C, E to 50th Street

The Time is a modern boutique hotel with clean, brightly-coloured rooms and some great in-room features, including web television.

TRUMP INTERNATIONAL HOTEL AND TOWER
1 Central Park West at Columbus Circle
212-299-1000
fax 212-299-1150
www.trumpintl.com
Subway A, C, B, D, 1, 9 to 59th Street - Columbus Circle.

Donald Trump's skyscraper of a hotel offers serious opulence. It just does suites, which is one of the reasons why prices are high. But you do get a personal assistant and chef.

WALDORF-ASTORIA
301 Park Avenue at 50th Street
212-355-3000
fax: 212-872-7272
www.waldorf.com
Subway E, F to Lexington Ave; 6 to 51st St.

This very famous landmark hotel used to be the world's largest. Associated with celebrity and wealth, the hotel has recently been restored to its former glory.

Coming to America

Check This Out

Check out this guide, which covers everything you need to know about New York City once you have landed. These pages tell you what to do to stay healthy, how to make the most of your dollars, and advise you about sex in the city. Find out when it's hot, when the parties are, and how to generally stay out of trouble in the Big Bad Apple,

Getting There

ARRIVING BY AIR

New York has three airports: JFK, La Guardia and Newark. All equally tiresome to get to and from and used by all major airlines.

How to Reach the City from JFK

The AirTrain that's due for completion in 2003 is hoped to make a 45-minute journey to Midtown a possibility. Meanwhile, your options are subway, taxi or bus. Call 718-244-4444 for travel info from JFK.

SUBWAY

It's supposed to take 60–75 minutes from Howard Beach to Manhattan, but that doesn't include the 30-minute bus ride to get to the station to get the A-train into town. Hop on the free bus (it should be yellow, white and blue),

making sure it's for Howard Beach, then make sure your A-train is going to Rockways, not Ozone Park-Lefferts Blvd. It will cost you just $1.50, but you've been warned – it's arduous and not recommended late at night.

BUS

NEW YORK AIRPORT SERVICE

A 60–75-minute trip into town (depending on traffic, which at rush hour is start-stop all the way to Manhattan), stopping at Grand Central, Port Authority and Penn Station, will cost you $13. From 6am to 1pm they're every half hour, after that every 15 minutes until 11.40pm.

EXPRESS SHUTTLE USA

Again 60–75 minutes, this time to any Midtown hotel, these buses run every 20 minutes and cost $14. To order a bus to take you back to the airport, check your hotel doesn't already have an arrangement, or ring 212-315-

3006 or 212-757-6840, making sure you leave a good hour for it to get to you.

SUPER SHUTTLE

This around-the-clock service will take you 60-75 minutes and will cost you $19 for the first person, $9 for each additional person travelling with you. The only bummer with this is that the driver will wait until he has a full complement of passengers before he sets off. Ring 212-258-3826.

TAXI

Be prepared to queue and travel in a very grimy car, probably with a driver whose grasp of the English language could leave a lot to be desired. Your journey will take you around an hour, and there is supposed to be a $33 flat fare plus $3.50 for tolls, though some of the taxi drivers will try it on. Only get a taxi from the official queue, where an attendant is usually on duty to advise you how much it's going to cost. Don't be daunted by the queue – it moves pretty quickly. If you decide to share a cab into town, the meter will start running when you've made your first set down.

How to Reach the City from Newark

Further out, but marginally nicer and just as easy (if slightly more expensive) to get to and from, Newark is now an even busier airport than JFK. The AirTrain is nearing completion, but no one is quite sure when it should be ready for paying punters. In the

meantime, you have the usual bus and taxi options.

Call 973-961-6000 for general travel info from Newark.

BUS

As with JFK, Express Shuttle USA operates from Newark, as does Olympia Airport Express, which will drop you off outside Penn Station, Grand Central Terminal and Wall Street. Fares are from $11–$14, and they leave every 15 or so minutes.

TAXI

A taxi from Newark will cost you approx $40, plus tolls and tips.

How to Reach the City from La Guardia

BUS AND TAXI

Grab an M60 bus for $1.50, which will take you to Broadway at 106th Street. Depending on how busy the traffic is, it should take about 30 minutes. New York Airport Service Express Bus and Express Shuttle USA also run every 20 or so minutes and cost between $10 and $13. A yellow cab from La Guardia will cost about $25 plus tolls and tip. Call 718-533-3400 for general info from La Guardia.

PASSPORTS AND VISAS

Visitors from the UK, the EU (apart from Ireland, Portugal, the Vatican City and Greece) and

Japan can all travel without a visa to the US under the visa waiver scheme, as long as the stay does not exceed 90 days. You'll need a valid passport, an open or return ticket, and to fill in a green form.

CUSTOMS AND IMMIGRATION

If you're used to wafting through customs in Europe, be prepared to wait in the longest line you ever saw. Having filled in your customs and immigration forms during your flight, you have to queue to present them with your passport to an immigration official. Fill the forms in carefully, as they are very picky and serious about this element. You may have to explain the nature of your visit. Don't worry about it: they ask everyone a couple of questions, and may even look you up on the computer, so no wonder it takes so long. They are even more thorough if you don't have that return ticket.

WHAT YOU'RE PERMITTED TO TAKE INTO THE US

If you're over 21, you are allowed to bring up to $100 worth of gifts before you become eligible to pay tax ($400 worth for US citizens),

one carton of 200 cigarettes or 100 cigars, and one litre of alcohol. If you're going to bring cigars in, make sure they're not Cuban, as they'll be taken from you. Don't take any plants, fruit, meat or fresh produce either. Immigrant Assistance Line: 414–543–6767 (Mon–Fri 9.30am–5pm).

WHAT YOU'RE PERMITTED TO BRING BACK TO THE UK

200 cigarettes; or 100 cigarillos; or 50 cigars; or 250g of tobacco; 2 litres of still table wine; 1 litre of spirits or strong liqueurs over 22% volume; or 2 litres fortified wine, sparkling wine or other liqueurs; 60cc/ml of perfume, 250cc/ml of toilet water. £145 worth of other goods, including gifts and souvenirs.

People under 17 are not entitled to the tobacco or alcohol allowance for obvious reasons.

If you intend bringing something back into the UK worth more than the limit of £145, you will have to pay charges on the full value of the item, not just on the value above £145.

IMMIGRATION ATTITUDES TO HIV-POSITIVE PEOPLE

It was ironically the Clinton administration that passed laws in 1993 which can bar entry to anyone diagnosed as HIV-positive. Non-US citizens who are HIV-positive are not eligible for a visa and if you do tick the box that states you have a communicable disease on the visa waiver form, immigration officials do, in theory, have the right to refuse you entry. It's a long shot, but if confronted about HIV medications, you

Liquor

might want to be prepared to tell officials you have another non-communicable complaint. Ask your doctor or clinic for advice.

In the City

TOURIST OFFICES AND INFORMATION

NEW YORK CITY'S OFFICIAL VISITOR INFORMATION CENTER

ℹ️ 810 Seventh Ave at 53rd Street

📞 212-484-1222 www.nycvisit.com

🕐 Mon–Fri 8.30am–6pm; Sat–Sun 9am–5pm.

TIMES SQUARE VISITORS CENTER

ℹ️ 1560 Broadway at 46th Street

📞 212-768-1560

🕐 8am–8pm every day.

At both these centres you'll find the usual leaflets on visitor attractions and accommodation, free maps and discount coupons. You get the usual good level of New York Service.

PUBLIC TRANSPORT

SUBWAY

New York's subway is nowhere near as scary as it used to be and is so cheap and fast that you're best just biting the bullet and finding out that it's really OK.

The subway runs 24 hours a day, though after midnight you'll get a reduced service (making it advisable to hop into a cab), and is cheap, with just a $1.50 flat fare. You can usually spot entrances to the subway by green globes, though you should check that not only is it

good for the line you want but also for the direction, as uptown and downtown trains usually have different entrances. If you see a red globe, do look carefully – it means the station is not always open.

Use the machines in subway stations to buy your token (a little brass coin that works on subways and buses), and dump all those quarters and dimes that have been building up in your pockets. You can use a credit or debit card. Machines take notes, but if you're having any trouble there are usually sales booths as well.

The best way to feel like a native is to buy a MetroCard, which come in two varieties: pay-as-you-use or unlimited ride, which are good for a day ($4), seven days ($17) or 30 days ($63). You can get MetroCards from the machines or from some newsagents and supermarkets. You can use your MetroCard on the subway and on the bus, and don't think you're being really clever by buying one between two: they've thought of that and have made them function only once every 18 minutes. The spin-off is that you get a free transfer ride if you re-use it within two hours. Just put your token or MetroCard into the slot and the barriers open for you.

The system can seem a bit complicated as different trains pull into the same platforms. Check your subway map carefully to see that the line you want – it'll be called either a number or a letter – starts where you're starting and finishes where you want to finish. And when the train comes in, check the letter or number on the side of it. You don't want to go jumping on an Express train when only the Local train is going to stop at your destination.

Ready to ride the subway

TAXIS

Those yellow cabs look glamorous, but be warned, New York taxis are mostly fairly degenerate. Not only is there not much in the way of leg room with a big old Perspex screen coming down between you and the driver, but the plastic seats are often ripped and the floors not too clean or tidy. The celebrity seatbelt safety messages are amusing, though.

Hail only cabs that have their light on, and make sure you're in there before you start discussing your destination. If you want to go to Brooklyn or Queens, insist: he has to take you there. Give your destination in terms of cross streets (so, Eighth Avenue with 12th Street) and have some sort of idea where you're going, as sometimes they won't. Cabs fit four people, but that's based on someone sitting up front with your driver.

On the bright side, cabs are plentiful (except when it's raining) and fairly cheap, costing $2 plus 30 cents per fifth of a mile with a 50–cent supplement after 8pm, which means that hopping around Manhattan you'll never run up that high a fare, though be prepared to pop an extra dollar on top for the driver. And pay him before you get out.

If you do have any complaints to make, take the driver's name. There should be a card with his photo, name and number on display. Get your automated receipt, which has a meter number on it, and ring the Taxi and Limousine Commission on 212-676-1000 (the number's in the cab) between 9am and 5pm weekdays. All cabs are no-smoking by law, so don't light up.

The city is full of yellow cabs

When you phone for a taxi, agree the fare before they send anyone. And get in a dodgy cab at your peril – it could just be mobile muggers for all you know.

USEFUL NUMBERS

Tel Aviv 1-800-222-9888/777-7777

Downtown Delancey Car Service 228-3301

BUSES

New York buses are cleaner and nicer than taxis and the drivers usually absolutely charming. Add to that the fact that on most routes you'll never have to wait much longer than five minutes and you'll find it a great way to get around and still see the city.

Buy a MetroCard or have tokens (see Subway section) or have the exact $1.50 as the driver doesn't do change. You just drop your token or coins in the slot by the driver or slide your MetroCard in yourself, the driver does nothing but invigilate. Find the bus stop (they are usually every couple of blocks and look out for the yellow kerbs as a clue) and when your bus comes put out your hand. If you need to make a connection, ask for a transfer ticket, which you have to use within two hours.

Some buses are LED – look for 'Limited' in the front window – and only stop at major stops. When your stop is coming up, press the strip (there should be a sign to indicate the bus driver is ready to stop) and, if you're going out the back door, remember to give it a hefty shove – and the driver a shout if he's forgotten to open it.

CAR HIRE

New York is far from a driver's paradise, with the volatility of other drivers, poor parking and streets with great big holes in them just a few of the reasons why you should stick to cabs and buses and subways. If you're intent on hiring – maybe you want to drive out to the Hamptons – there are some very serious dos and don'ts.

Metres will cost you 25 cents from 20 minutes to an hour. If you get yourself towed away, ring 1-718-422-7800 and get your $150 ready.

If you're still keen, make sure you have a major credit card, passport and driver's licence, and be prepared to pay $50–$75 per day, with fares skyrocketing around holidays, and fork out for the most comprehensive insurance package on offer. You may have to be 25 years of age, but always ask.

Do's and Don'ts

Never, ever park within 50 feet of a fire hydrant: they will haul your wheels before you've even stepped out of the car.

Never drive faster than 30 miles per hour.

Never speed past a stopped school bus; they'll fine you.

Never turn right on a red light.

Never go without your seatbelt or allow your passengers to do so.

Never park on the side of the street that is being cleared for cleaning. It's complicated: read all signs

USEFUL NUMBERS

A1 Value 212-348-5151

Avis 1-800-230-4898 www.avis.com

Budget 1-800-527-0700 www.budget.com

Enterprise 1-800-325-8007

Hertz 1-800-654-3131

CLIMATE

NYC is something of an all-year-round city, but it gets pretty sweltering in the summer (well, it is on a level with Madrid) and freezing and snowy in the winter.

The best times of year to go are definitely late spring/early summer and from September onwards. Christmas time is always special, but it can snow quite heavily.

CLIMATE AVERAGES

	Temp	Rainfall cm
January	0	8.1
February	0.8	7.9
March	5.2	10.7
April	11.2	9.7
May	17	9.7
June	21.9	8.1
July	25	9.7
August	24	10.2
September	21	9.4
October	14.2	8.6
November	8.3	9.9
December	2.6	9.7

TELEPHONING

Use your hotel phone at your own peril. They will charge you through the nose just for dialling, never mind if anyone picks up or if you are using a phone card. In call boxes you can use quarters or dimes – local calls are 25 cents for the first three minutes – or the handy phone card in denominations starting at $5, available from most stores, which is a must if you're phoning home. With a phone card, just follow the instructions printed on the back. You get charged $1 or $1.50 connection fee followed by cheap chat, which makes them ideal for long distance, ridiculous for local calls. You can also use your credit card for phoning by dialling AT&T on freefone 1-800 225 5288.

Manhattan numbers all start with 212. Make sure you don't dial 212 if you are dialling from within the 212 area. There are new Manhattan codes 646 and 917, so don't be surprised to see those. If you are dialling outside your area, add a 1 before the area code.

For directory enquiries, where you can also get addresses, ring 411 free from payphones. The operator is reached on 0 – for the international operator or enquiries.

If you are phoning home, you need to dial 011 first.

INTERNATIONAL DIALLING CODES

Australia 61
Canada dial the long distance combination of 1+area code+telephone number.
New Zealand 64
Republic of Ireland 353
UK 44

BIKE HIRE

Take your life in your hands and make sure you have the right insurance and that the bike you hire has a bell (you can get fined if it hasn't).

Keep in touch

USEFUL NUMBERS

Bicycles Plus $7.50 per hour/$25 per day, 2nd Avenue at 87th Street, 212-722-2201; Metro Bike $7 per hour/$45 per day, 14th Street between 1st and 2nd Aves 212-228-4344; 1311 Lexington Avenue at 88th Street. 212-427-4450; Sixth Avenue at 15th Street, 212-255-5100; 417 Canal Street, 212-334-8000

EMBASSIES AND CONSULATES

Australia 212-351-6500

Canada 212-596-1700

New Zealand 212-832-4038

Republic of Ireland 212-319-2555

UK 212-745-0200

POLICE AND CRIME

Crime in New York City has plummeted in recent years, making it – amazingly – one of the safer cities in the US.Call the police on 911 (the same number applies for ambulance and fire service). New York's finest have a bit of a reputation for toughness, but for a tourist they will no doubt be on their best behaviour and, though they may not be thought of as the most gay-friendly citizens of NYC, as New Yorkers they will no doubt have seen it all before, so don't hesitate to contact them. For support when dealing with the police, contact the NYC Gay and Lesbian Anti-Violence Project on their 24-hour hotline: 212-714-1141.

If you are the victim of a crime make sure you get a crime number from the police for insurance.

As far as avoiding crime goes, you need to take the same precautions you would in any other city in the world: be sensible when walking around – especially

at night – stick to places where there are other people, don't flaunt your valuables, and don't get so out of it you don't know what's going on. And if you're going out in an out-of-the-way place, ask the man on the door how to call a cab.

Crime can happen anywhere in New York City, but the areas you are most likely to feel least safe – rightly or wrongly – are the Lower East Side, up in Spanish Harlem and Harlem proper and in the Outer Boroughs. Eighth Avenue in Midtown is also pretty sleazy day and night.

As far as common scams are concerned, if you find yourself being offered an unbelievable bargain, especially from a box in the street, be prepared to be fleeced. It's not unknown for someone to buy a lovely new ghetto blaster to get home and find a box filled with bricks.

DRINK AND DRUGS

DRINKING

It may be flattering to be asked for identification to get into a drinking establishment when you're 45, but don't risk it. You have to be 21 to drink in New York and their licence depends on making sure you are, so wear something you can fit your passport into.

DRUGS

Maybe once upon a time New York was drugs central, but the days of being off-it NYC are over. Under Mayor Giuliani, clubs have become so paranoid about being closed down over drugs that they just aren't freely available and obviously carry very heavy

The city that never sleeps

penalties. You'd have to be crazy, frankly. As far as smoking goes, New York is not California and you are allowed to smoke in public, though most people don't.

HEALTH

Don't even think of going to New York without insurance. Public health care is skimpy (and, trust us, you wouldn't like it anyway), while private health care is famously expensive. You can also be drawn into a costly lawsuit if any of your behaviour accidentally causes injury. So, get that insurance and make sure it covers everything bar watersports and skiing.

HIV as a 'Pre-Existing Condition' for Travel Insurance: HIV and HIV-related illnesses may be considered pre-existing if the condition is not 'stable' 60 days prior to the purchase of insurance. It makes covering yourself difficult, as any change in medication or progress of the condition can be used to deny coverage. Some policies treat HIV as a pre-existing condition, whether your treatment and state of health are stable or not, which means that they would not pay out for cancellation or medical assistance in case of an HIV-related incident. Your other health cover needs – accidents, injury – would not be affected.

There exists such a thing as a Pre-Existing Conditions Waiver, which many travel insurers offer, but you do need to see it in black and white on your certificate of insurance. If you want to find out exactly what is covered, you need to get in touch with the insurer (and that doesn't mean the travel agent where you bought the policy), but beware that even if they reassure you over the phone, if it isn't in the policy, then it doesn't hold water.

HOW TO DEAL WITH A HEALTH CRISIS

You can get seen at a number of walk-in clinics in New York if a health concern crops up. Be prepared to pay over the counter (from $75 up), though the cost is usually redeemable against your insurance policy.

D.O.C.S CLINICS

📍 55 East 34th Street
📞 212-252-6000.
🕐 Mon–Thu 8am–8pm; Fri 8am–7pm; Sat 9am–3pm; Sun 9am–2pm
📍 1555 Third Ave 212-828-2300
📍 202 West 23rd Street 212-352-2600

IN CASE OF EMERGENCY

In case of real emergency, call 911.

If you require emergency treatment, awful as it sounds, you first have to contact the emergency number on your insurance to find out which emergency room you should go to.

You will probably be expected to pay up front yourself and then reclaim later, so take your credit card.

24-HOUR EMERGENCY ROOMS

📍 Bellevue Hospital, First Avenue at East 27th Street 212-562-4141
📍 Mount Sinai Hospital, 100 Madison Avenue between 99th and 100 Streets 212-241-7171
📍 New York Presbyterian Hospital, 510

East 70th Street at York Avenue
212-746-5050
📍 St Vincent's Hospital, Seventh Avenue between 11th and 12th Streets
212-604-7997

DOCTORS

Doctor on Call provides 24-hour house calls. Call 212-737-2333.

VACCINATIONS

Vaccinations are not necessary for New York.

24-HOUR PHARMACIES

There are 24-hour pharmacies open all over town, but some drugs will require a prescription including certain preparations available over the counter in the UK such as herpes treatment Zovirax.

📍 Duane Reade, 224 West 57th Street at Broadway; Broadway at 91st Street 212-541-9708; 1279 Third Avenue at 74th Street 212-744-2668; 485 Lexington Avenue at 47th Street 212-682-5338.
📍 Rite Aid run a number of 24-hour pharmacies. Call 800-RITE-AID for details of the nearest branch.

HIV AND SAFE SEX

Take all the precautions you would take at home, and maybe more. It's easy to get carried away with holiday sex, but condoms are easy to come by so there's really no excuse not to be safe.

GAY GROUPS AND RESOURCES

THE LESBIAN & GAY COMMUNITY SERVICES CENTER

📍 1 Little West 12th Street between Greenwich and Hudson Streets
📞 212-620-7310; www.gaycenter.org

This multi-storey centre over in the meatpacking district is the bottom line in support centres. A huge ramshackle affair, it's a great place for loading up on leaflets and getting any specialised information you might need.

MICHAEL CALLEN-AUDRE LORDE COMMUNITY HEALTH CENTER

356 West 18th Street between 8th and 9th Aves

212-271-7200; www.callen-lorde.org

A huge lesbian and gay health centre where you can discuss any health issues and be directed to the right help and medication.

GAY & LESBIAN SWITCHBOARD OF NEW YORK

212-989-0999; www.glnh.org; Mon–Fri 4pm–midnight; Sat noon–5pm

Call if you have a crisis you need to talk through.

GAY LIFE IN THE CITY

Don't forget that 11 October is National Coming Out Day. Do what you have to do.

BASTILLE DAY FESTIVAL

A new meatpacking event popular with the local drag community based around Florent, the restaurant in Gansevoort Street on or around 14th July.

CIRCUIT PARTIES

The now infamous Black Party and White Party, set up to commemorate the passing of the legendary Saint nightclub, are two events gay men are willing to fly across the world to attend. The Black Party – a fetish night – is usually held the third weekend in March and costs $100 (in cash!) on the door, though cheaper tickets are available in advance. Arrive after midnight and stay till the next afternoon. The White Party – a less heavy alternative – is in February and costs between $65 and $85. Check www.saintatlarge.com to find out dates and details.

GAY AND LESBIAN PRIDE MARCH

During the last weekend in June, the March, which starts at Columbus Circle near Central Park and goes right down Fifth Avenue, commemorates the Stonewall riots that started the gay rights movement. It attracts hundreds of thousands of whistle-blowing gay men, lesbians, bisexuals, transsexuals, you name it. The parade ends, appropriately enough, on Christopher Street, near the site of those riots, where you can join in PrideFest, a fair on Washington Street between Christopher and Spring Streets. The town's bars and clubs obviously don't let the date go by without their own celebrations, and there is a huge Annual Pride Dance by the Hudson at 13th Street. There is an AIDS Candlelight Vigil held the Friday before the celebrations, and a Leather Pride the weekend before. Check listings magazines for details.

NEW YORK LESBIAN AND GAY FILM FESTIVAL

Phone 212-254-8504 or check www.newfestival.org/ for details of the next Festival, usually held in June or July. There is also a New York Lesbian and Gay Experimental

Film and Video Festival held in September.

ST PATRICK'S DAY PARADE

If you are of an argumentative state of mind, you could attend the St. Patrick's Day parade on 17th March to protest at the continued ban on gay groups joining the parade.

MEDIA

There really is no shortage of gay media in New York, most of it free. For general bar listings and disco details, get yourself a copy of *HX* or *Next*, both up for grabs in bars and clubs. Also look for the gay freebie *Metro*. For a more general idea of what's going on, including cinema and theatre listings, you can get your free copy of the legendary *Village Voice* (look out for pull-down dispensers on street corners or check record stores) and make a bee-line for Michael Musto's column to find out the latest gay gossip. *Time Out New York* is also an excellent magazine, dealing with eating, drinking, clubbing and entertainment in NYC. It has a great Gay & Lesbian section. For a whole range of gay freebies, including publications for the HIV-positive, go to the Lesbian & Gay Community Services Center.

CURRENCY, CREDIT CARDS AND BANKS

Be careful with American bank-notes, as they all look a bit the same, and even the coins are tricky, as some of the bigger ones are worth more than the smaller ones. One dollar equals 100 cents. The

Find out what's on this week

This way, sir

coins are copper one cents or pennies (1c), silver nickels (5c), silver dimes (10c, smaller than nickels), quarters (25c) and the new one-dollar coin ($1). Notes come in the following denominations: $1, $5, $10, $20, $50 and $100. The $100 bill is not accepted in some smaller establishments.

The major credit cards are accepted by most hotels, shops and restaurants – in fact, some hotels and other establishments won't take your reservation without them.

TIME

Eastern Standard Time is five hours behind GMT.

ELECTRICITY

The voltage in the US is 110- 120V 60-cycle AC and the plugs flat-pin, so you'll definitely need an adaptor for UK appliances. Get one at the airport

TIPPING

Tipping is a way of life in the States, and you ignore it at your peril. It may seem cheeky to have to pay 15–20% on top of every meal you have, but just think of it as what keeps the high level of service there.

Hotel porters will usually expect a dollar or two per bag. In taxis work out 15–20%, or just leave an extra dollar if it's a short ride. And, weirdest of all for non-Americans, don't forget that in bars you are expected to leave a dollar per drink – even though you went up and got it yourself.

PUBLIC HOLIDAYS

Although Americans only get a couple of weeks of paid holiday per year, they do get an inordinate amount of public holidays.

1 January	New Year's Day
3rd Monday in January	Martin Luther King Day
12 February	Lincoln's Birthday
3rd Monday in February	Washington's Birthday or President's Day
Easter Sunday	
Last Monday in May	Memorial Day or Decoration Day
4 July	Independence Day
1st Monday in September	Labor Day
2nd Monday in October	Columbus Day
11 November	Veterans' Day
4th Thursday in November	Thanksgiving
25 December	Christmas Day

The stars and the stripes

INDEX

INDEX

 **NOTEBOOK**

CONTACT LIST

Name _____

Address _____

_____

_____

Tel _____

Fax _____

email _____

Name _____

Address _____

_____

_____

Tel _____

Fax _____

email _____

Name _____

Address _____

_____

_____

Tel _____

Fax _____

email _____

Name _____

Address _____

_____

_____

Tel _____

Fax _____

email _____

Name _____

Address _____

_____

_____

Tel _____

Fax _____

email _____

Name _____

Address _____

_____

_____

Tel _____

Fax _____

email _____

CONTACT LIST

Name

Address

Tel

Fax

email

Name

Address

Tel

Fax

email

Name

Address

Tel

Fax

email

Name

Address

Tel

Fax

email

Name

Address

Tel

Fax

email

Name

Address

Tel

Fax

email

CONTACT LIST

Name

Address

Tel

Fax

email

Name

Address

Tel

Fax

email

Name

Address

Tel

Fax

email

Name

Address

Tel

Fax

email

Name

Address

Tel

Fax

email

Name

Address

Tel

Fax

email

MY TOP RESTAURANTS

Fill in details of your favourite restaurants below . . .
Tell us about them by logging on to **www.outaround.com**

Restaurant _____

Contact Details _____

Comments _____

Restaurant _____

Contact Details _____

Comments _____

Restaurant _____

Contact Details _____

Comments _____

My Top Restaurants

MY TOP BARS

Fill in details of your favourite bars below . . .
Tell us about them by logging on to **www.outaround.com**

My Top Bars

Bar

Contact Details

Comments

Bar

Contact Details

Comments

Bar

Contact Details

Comments

Fill in details of your favourite clubs below . . .
Tell us about them by logging on to *www.outaround.com*

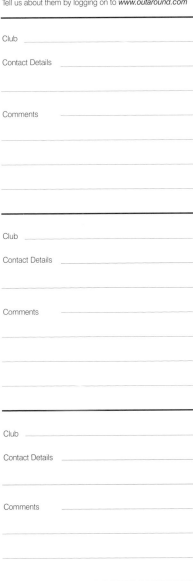

Club

Contact Details

Comments

Club

Contact Details

Comments

Club

Contact Details

Comments

AMSTERDAM

LONDON

MIAMI

NEW YORK

PARIS

SAN FRANCISCO

Please help us update future editions by taking part in our reader survey. Every returned form will be acknowledged and to show our appreciation we will send you a voucher entitling you to £1 off your next Out Around guide or any other Thomas Cook guidebook ordered direct from Thomas Cook Publishing. Just take a few minutes to complete this form and return it to us.

Alternatively you can visit www.Outaround.com and email us the answers to the questions using the numbers given below.

We'd also be glad to hear of your comments, updates or recommendations on places we cover or you think that we ought to cover.

1 Which Out Around guide did you purchase?

2 Have you purchased other Out Around guides in the series?

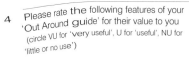

☐ Yes ☐ No   If Yes, please specify

3 Which of the following tempted you into buying your Out Around guide. (Please tick as appropriate)

☐ The price
☐ The rainbow spine
☐ The cover
☐ The fact it was a dedicated gay travel guide
☐ Other

4 Please rate the following features of your 'Out Around guide' for their value to you (circle VU for 'very useful', U for 'useful', NU for 'little or no use')

'A Day Out' features	VU	U	NU
Top Sights	VU	U	NU
Top restaurants and cafés and listings	VU	U	NU
Top shops and listings	VU	U	NU
Top hotels and listings	VU	U	NU
Top clubs and bars and listings	VU	U	NU
Theatre and music venues	VU	U	NU
Gyms and sauna choices	VU	U	NU
Practical information	VU	U	NU

FEEDBACK FORM

Feedback Form

5 How did you book your holiday?

☐ Package deal
☐ Package deal through a gay-specific tour operator
☐ Flight only
☐ Accommodation only
☐ Flight and accommodation booked separately

6 How many people are travelling in your party?

7 Which other cities do you intend to/have travelled to in the next/past 12 months?

Amsterdam   Yes ☐   No ☐
London   Yes ☐   No ☐
Miami   Yes ☐   No ☐
New York   Yes ☐   No ☐
Paris   Yes ☐   No ☐
San Francisco Yes ☐   No ☐
Other (please specify)

8 Please use this space to tell us about any features that in your opinion could be changed, improved, or added in future editions of the book, or any other comments you would like to make concerning the book:

_____
_____
_____
_____
_____

From time to time we send our readers details of new titles or special offers. Please tick here if you wish your name to be held on our mailing list (Note: our mailing list is never sold to other companies). ☐

Please detach this page and send it to: The Editor, Out Around, Thomas Cook Publishing, PO Box 227, The Thomas Cook Business Park, Peterborough PE3 8XX, United Kingdom.

9 Your age category
☐ under 21 ☐ 21-30 ☐ 31-40 ☐ 41-50 ☐ 51+

First name (or initials)
_____

Last name
_____

Your full address (Please include postal or zip code)
_____
_____
_____

Your daytime telephone number:
_____